What ot

Gosp ormation

I am deeply grateful for Dale Ratzlaff's understanding of, and love for, God's gospel which shines on every page of this little book. By taking us into a consideration of the great words of the gospel and by reminding us of the wonderful truth of our union with Christ, he not only increases our understanding of God's work on our behalf, he deepens our love for Christ. Christians are good news people. We are created by the gospel, and are called to be centered on and shaped by it. Our calling is to be gospel people, good news people who believe, guard, proclaim, and embody the gospel. God's Word tells us that as we behold the glory of the Lord we are being transformed by the Spirit into the image of Christ. The gospel is sufficient to save us and powerful to transform us. Dale's book is a God-given aid to enable us to behold the glory of our Lord Jesus in the gospel and thus to experience *Gospel Transformation*.

Gary Inrig, D. Min., Th. M., Redlands, California

Gospel Transformation is a positive and humble explanation of the divine work of God in redemption and sanctification through the power of God. The book illustrates that salvation is the inflow and outflow of the wonderful grace of God who saves us from sin and its wages. This book is needed everywhere the name of Jesus Christ is preached so that the true gospel will shine out and above all false teachings which darken the council of God.

Andre R. Hill, Ph.D.,
Education Ministry Literacy Coordinator, Jamaica

I really enjoyed *Gospel Transformation* and found it to be a great analysis of the salvation process. It is such a basic function of being a Christian that it is often taken for granted. When you take the gospel step by step you see the importance of understanding God's work in our lives, the power of His grace, and what saving faith looks like. I loved the focus on being "in Christ" and the importance of knowing the impact this has on our life. This has been a transforming part of my life. It gets me pumped being reminded of who I am "In Christ." I believe this will be a book that transcends the Adventist world and will be read and enjoyed by all Christians. Great work in your "old age"!

Dan Burton, Missions Chair, Waverley Baptist Church, Winnipeg, Manitoba, Canada

I grew up as a Seventh-day Adventist and attended Adventist schools through my Master's degree at PUC, I taught in the Adventist system for 42 years so I am very familiar with salvation by the grace of God with a "but". "If you want to spend eternity in heaven then believe in Christ, but you have to stop beating your wife, but don't tell lies, and be sure to keep the 7th day Sabbath holy." Christ, when on earth did NOT say "believe in me and keep the Sabbath and thou shalt be saved." He only said "believe in me." Dale has done a marvelous job of unpacking this concept of "belief," documenting it from the books of the New Testament and making it understandable. I have not only been blessed by this reading, but my faith in Christ and my assurance of salvation have grown. I strongly recommend *Gospel Transformation* for those who want to know and understand God's grace and the full concept of belief.

Gilbert J. Muth, Ph.D., Professor Emeritus of Biology, Pacific Union College, Angwin, California

Gospel Transformation helps me understand that I am not only counted righteous but am a genuine child of God and am entitled to all the privileges and benefits He offers His children now and forever. I like that it includes lots of Scripture and that there are enough Greek explanations in the text so that one can discuss the issues. The book also gives me enough ammunition to more thoroughly discuss the issue of "cheap grace". This is a great primer for those who are new to the concept of the simple gospel and also a joyful affirmation for those who have rested in Christ for years.

Richard Regester, Elder, Seventh-day Adventist Church,
Green Forest, Arkansas

I studied *Gospel Transformation* and found it very refreshing. It takes a giant leap beyond the traditional pedantic approach of fossilized religion. This book opens the window into the realm of the Spirit where we begin to breathe the fresh air of revelation.

Sam Pestes, Retired Pastor,
Kelowna, BC, Canada

Dale, I have read your new book, *Gospel Transformation*. It is a spiritual blessing to see these truths put into a simple and yet systematic order so that anyone who has even a basic understanding of Scripture can understand these profound truths. I really liked your explanation about being baptized into Christ by the Holy Spirit. This concept has often been lost when one reads water baptism into Romans 6, instead of seeing that it is the work of the Holy Spirit whereby we identify with Him, whom to know is life eternal. You book is really needed in the Philippines. So many pastors here have been taught about works righteousness, sacramentalism, and old traditions, instead of the simple gospel of faith in Christ.

Pastor Verle Streifling, Ph.D., Iloilo City, Philippines

I highly recommend *Gospel Transformation.* In a clear, concise and easy to understand manner Dale carefully leads the reader to the proper biblical meaning of what it is to be "in Christ", thereby breaking the shackles of religious legalism and spiritual bondage. I enjoyed this refreshing book from cover to cover, particularly from the beginning where he dedicates this book to his own sons, their wives, and his four grandchildren, demonstrating the kind of love he has put into this work. The final two chapters of the book are worth the price of the book because here Dale succinctly outlines what it means to have a "gospel transformation" by being "in Christ." May the Lord use this book for His glory and give spiritual freedom to those who are now suffering under the weight of their own imperfect acts of righteousness, rather than resting in what Christ has already accomplished through His perfect sacrifice for sins at Calvary.

Larry Wessels, Director, Christian Answers,
Christian Debater, Austin, Texas

I highly recommend *Gospel Transformation* to anyone who wants to have the assurance of salvation in the mercy and grace of our Savior, Jesus Christ. Too often we try to add our own works to the finished work of Christ. Our human tendency is to think that if we are just good enough, or if we would keep a certain day, or refrain from this or that, we will be saved—as if we can help our great God do a work that is already finished through His Son. The Bible clearly teaches that it is the finished work of Christ and our faith in His sacrifice for sins that assures our salvation. Dale has clearly outlined this truth in his new book. Being "in Christ" is the only way we can be transformed into new creatures and this book helps us to know how to do this. This is a great resource for anyone who is willing to study the Bible and humbly submit to its truths.

Darlene Bieber Hanson, Event Project Administrator,
The Well Community Church, Fresno, California

I have just finished *Gospel Transformation*. What a blessing this book is to me and I'm sure will be to many other readers. I believe those from a Seventh-day Adventist background appreciate the gospel more than many Christians who may take it for granted. I plan to read this book over and over and over to remind me of the "in Christ" status that I seem to forget sometimes. This book will be a wonderful blessing to all who read it and absorb the principles you teach. God bless you and I will pray that this book will be able to be read by thousands of people.

Jim E. Duncan, Compass Church, Bend Oregon

About the Author

Dale Ratzlaff was a conservative, fourth generation Seventh-day Adventist (SDA). He pastored three SDA churches, and taught Bible in an Adventist school for seven years. Each year he took his Bible Doctrines class through the first eight chapters of Romans. This resulted in a more accurate and deeper understanding of the gospel. From that time on the gospel with all the ramifications emanating from this glorious truth has been the center piece and driving force of his ministry.

While nearing the end of his doctoral program at Andrews University, he became convinced that the SDA doctrine of the investigative judgment and cleansing of the heavenly sanctuary could not be supported by Scripture, was contrary to clear biblical teaching, and undermined the new covenant gospel of grace that he had discovered in his study of Romans. Pastor Ratzlaff with his wife Carolyn, who was a denominationally employed Bible worker, left the SDA church at that time. Ratzlaff has pastored three evangelical churches, authored five books and has dozens of published articles.

In 2000 Dale and Carolyn Ratzlaff, working with Richard and Colleen Tinker, started Life Assurance Ministries, Inc., a non-profit corporation that publishes *Proclamation!*[1] a 32 page, full color journal, which at this writing is sent free of charge to approximately 30,000 homes. This has been a faith ministry from its inception.

Ratzlaff also manages LAM Publications, LLC, which publishes and sells a number of books on Adventist issues and the gospel. These combined ministries have helped thousands make the difficult transition from Adventism to healthy evangelical churches.

Ratzlaff believes the true, simple gospel of faith in Christ is central and sufficient. The gospel not only *saves* the soul, it also *transforms* the life. Therefore, the gospel must be defended in a spirit of love against legalistic compromises just as Paul defended it in the book of Galatians. It is his prayer that this little book will be used by God to clarify the apostolic gospel that was once for all delivered to the saints.

---

[1] www.LifeAssuranceMinistries.org

Gospel Transformation

—Saved by the gospel—
—Transformed by the gospel—

Dale Ratzlaff

LAM Publications, LLC
1042 North Powderhorn Road
Camp Verde, Arizona 86322

Dale@Ratzlaf.com
www.Ratzlaf.com
www.LifeAssurnaceMinistries.com

Cover design by Richard Tinker

LAM Publications, LLC
1042 North Powderhorn Road
Camp Verde, Arizona 86322
928-554-1001
dale@ratzlaf.com
http://www.LifeAssuranceMinistries.com
http://www.Ratzlaf.com
http://www.SbadoenCristo.com

Library of Congress Control Number: 2015907583

ISBN 978-1-937948-06-1

Printed in the United States of America

Dedication

To our two Boys—Bruce and Mike,

their wives—Denise and Sandy,

and our four grandchildren—

Melissa, Leonard, Ericka and Kenny

An understanding of the gospel of grace with the resulting life transformation is the greatest gift we can give you. It is our prayer that this little book will help you better understand the riches of God's grace by which you are saved and the life-transforming power of the Holy Spirit that will fill your life with purpose, joy, and peace.

Love,

Dad and Mom,

Grandpa and Grandma

Contents

Preface

This little study falls loosely into two sections: (1) saved by the gospel and (2) transformed by the gospel. From my ministry to legalistic groups over the past 25 years I sense there is a great need to make the gospel of Christ crystal clear. Even in some evangelical churches the gospel is sometimes fuzzy or even misunderstood. We need to know *for sure* what we trust for our eternal life is the true saving gospel that was once for all delivered to the saints.

A second need for a correct understanding of the gospel is that when accurately defined the gospel itself will point out hidden errors that may be lurking unseen in the shadows of our belief system. Think of the gospel as a brilliant diamond. The glory emanating from the cross of Calvary is refracted by each of the theological words of the gospel: righteousness, justification, redemption, propitiation, reconciliation, substitution, and representation. Each flashes a fire of a different color. Studied together, they reflect the glorious rainbow of God's love, mercy, and grace. Like a searching laser each facet will highlight truth and expose error.

A third reason the gospel needs clarity is that when rightly *understoo*d and *applied* it will transform the life. There are many unanswered questions about how the truth of the gospel actually transforms the life of a Christian. Many suggest some kind of behavior modification needs to be made before a person can rest assured that he has truly been born again. Therefore many well-meaning disciplers will direct new or even seasoned Christians to a list of disciplines—things to do or not do—designed to bring maturity into the Christin life. All too often the saving gospel is relegated to a past event and the focus of attention is taken off Christ and placed back on personal behavior as measured by the law. When this happens often doubt and a bewildering discouragement put a damper on the jubilant joy of one's "first love" experience with Christ.

I believe Scripture teaches that the Christian life is transformed when (1) we *thoroughly* understand the saving gospel, and (2) when we set our minds on things above by *affirming the biblical truths of the gospel,* namely the "in" and "with" Christ truths, the magnificent and precious promises, and the declarations made to true believers. When we take our eyes off our own personal behavior and focus on who we are "in" and "with" Christ *then* the Holy Spirit will work out the fruit of the Spirit in our lives.

> For what the Law could not do, weak as it was through the flesh, God *did*: sending His own Son in the likeness of sinful flesh and *as an offering* for sin, He condemned sin in the flesh, so that the requirement of the Law might be fulfilled in us, who do not walk according to the flesh but according to the Spirit. For those who are according to the flesh set their minds on the things of the flesh, but those who are according to the Spirit, the things of the Spirit (Rom. 8:3-5).

It is my prayer that you, the reader, will see a new beauty in the gospel as you view the various facets of this glorious truth. I believe you will experience true *gospel transformation* if you make it your *daily habit* to *affirm* who you *now are* "in" and "with" Christ and believe the magnificent and precious promises given to true believers.

I am indebted to Leon Morris' *The Epistle to the Romans*[2] and *The Apostolic Preaching of the*

---

[2] Leon Morris, *The Epistle To The Romans*, William B. Eerdmans Publishing Company, Grand Rapids, MI, 1988.

Cross,[3] and David K. Spurbeck Sr., *The Christian "in Christ"*[4] for some of the concepts in this book. Last but not least, I owe a debt of gratitude to my beloved Carolyn, wife of 58 years, for her helpful suggestions in preparing this book.

Throughout this book I have emphasized many words and phrases. These are my emphases and are designed to help the reader quickly grasp important points. I have at times referred to Greek verbs as these give insight, sometimes major insight, into various aspects of the gospel. For those not familiar with Greek I have listed the important point made by each usage. Bible quotations are from the New American Standard Bible (NASB), unless otherwise stated.

In His joy,

Dale Ratzlaff July, 2015

---

[3] Leon Morris, *The Apostolic Preaching of the Cross*, William B. Eerdmans Publishing Company, Grand Rapids, MI, 1965.

[4] David K. Spurbeck Sr., *The Christian "In Christ"*, Know to Grow "In Christ" Publications, Forest Grove, OR, 1999.

CHAPTER ONE

STARTING POINT

The gospel to which this book is dedicated is the saving activity of God in Christ. The "gospel" means good news. It is about what Christ has done for us by his life, death for sin, resurrection from the grave, and ascension to the Father's right hand. It is not good advice about what we must do.

Most would agree that the gospel of salvation is the central tenent of Christianity. However, as strange as it may seem, the gospel is often misunderstood, diluted with feel-good clichés, or loaded with heavy-weighted burdens. Sometimes it is just not clearly articulated and at others it is emasculated from its life-changing power. I loved the Lord Jesus and dedicated my life to Him as a young boy. I was a Christian for years but did not clearly understand the gospel nor did I have the assurance that I was fully accepted by God. I served as a pastor of several churches for a number of years and still did not understand the finer nuances of this glorious truth. My own understanding of the gospel has progressed in stages. At each stage I thought I understood it fully, that is until the next insight opened up new vistas that expanded my vision of the glorious grace of God. I have always had the desire to better understand the basis of my own assurance of salvation. At times I have experienced nagging questions the answers for which seemed very elusive. As my understanding of the gospel has grown, so has my love and dedication to the Lord. I have often prayed the Pauline prayer that I might "speak forth the mystery of Christ…that I may make it clear in the way I ought to speak."[5] And as I sit at my computer to start this book, my prayer is that we—both you and I—would not only better understand the gospel of our salvation but would enter into the ultimate experience Jesus predicted and promised in His last evening with His disciples.

The relationship within the Godhead

The unity of the Godhead, the mutual indwelling of the Father, Son, and Holy Spirit is a major theme of John's gospel and rightly so. This mutual

---

[5] Col. 4:3, 4.

indwelling and mutual dependence becomes the pattern for *all* relationships: God with God, God with man, and man with men. Jesus knew that important things must be repeated time and again.

> I and the Father are one (Jn.10:30).
>
> ...though you do not believe Me, believe the works, so that you may know and understand that the Father is in Me, and I in the Father (Jn. 10:38).

In John 14:6 Jesus tells His disciples that He is the "way, and the truth, and the life." Then He says,

> If you had known Me, you would have known My Father also; from now on you know Him and have seen Him.

To this Philip said, "Show us the Father..." Jesus answered:

> Have I been so long with you, and yet you have not come to know Me, Philip? He who has seen Me has seen the Father; how can you say, "Show us the Father"? Do you not believe that I am in the Father, and the Father is in Me? The words that I say to you I do not speak on My own initiative, but the Father abiding in Me does His works. Believe Me that I am in the Father and the Father is in Me; otherwise believe because of the works themselves (Jn. 14:9-11).

The interrelationship within the Godhead sets the pattern for believers

> I do not ask on behalf of these alone, but for those also who believe in Me [that means us!] through their word; that they may all be one; even as You, Father, are in Me and I in You, that **they also may be in Us**, so that the world may believe that You sent Me. The glory which You have given Me I have given to them, **that they may be one, just as We are one; I in them and You in Me, that they may be perfected in unity**, so that the world may know that You sent Me, and loved them, even as You have loved Me (Jn. 17:20-23).

The above paragraph from John 17 is perhaps the most profound statement in all of Scripture. That the Father, Son, and Holy Spirit can dwell "in us" and that we can dwell "in" the Father, Son, and Holy Spirit, opens up all kinds of questions and possibilities. Like the woman at the well we cry out "Lord, give me this water to drink!" How does all this happen? When does this happen? What are the results of this mutual indwelling? What is our part in this relationship and what is God's part? What are the benefits to us of being "in Christ"? How is Christ placed "into" us and what are the results of this mutual indwelling from God's perspective? How do all these relationships affect our relationship to other believers in Christ? Does this mutual indwelling take place in a moment of time or is this something that progresses from one stage to another?

My study leads me to believe these events all take place in a moment of time—the moment of salvation. However it often takes time, sometimes a long time, for us to actuate or experience the multitude of spiritual blessings that result from this event. Even though these events may take place in an instant, in order for us to understand the many facets of mutual indwelling we must study them in isolation and in the correct order. During the monsoon season in Arizona we sometimes get to see amazing light shows where the lightning sets the night sky ablaze with wonder. Even though a lightning strike happens in an instant, a careful observer can trace the direction of the flash. I believe it is the same way in our mutual indwelling relationships with God. Let us look at this one event in slow motion so we can better understand and appropriate the light of God's amazing grace—the rainbow of his grace and love. We now turn to the first step in this one event.

If you confess with your mouth Jesus as Lord, and believe in your heart that God raised Him from the dead, you will be saved

CHAPTER
Two

PLACED INTO CHRIST

Before a person can be placed into Christ it is necessary to realize that we are born outside of Christ. In Romans 1:18-3:20 Paul in no uncertain terms proves that gentiles, moralists, and law-keeping Jews are all under the wrath of God. We all sin in many ways, not only personally, but we are all counted as sinners because of the sin of the "one man" Adam.[6] We may think we are not that bad, but under the scrutiny of God's law interpreted by the Holy Spirit there is no escaping the fact of sin. Trying to hide our sin only reveals the depth of our wicked heart as Achan[7] and Ananias with his wife Sapphira[8] can attest.

---

[6] In Romans 5:12-20 Paul speaks of the sin of "one man" and "one transgression" that brought condemnation to all men. Studied in context this section shows that we are sinners, not only because of our personal sin, but we also participate in the sin of that "one man", Adam. In the same way, by "one act" of righteousness by "One Jesus Christ", justification results to all men when they believe.

[7] See Judges 6-7.

[8] See Acts 5:1-10.

Because of our sinful human nature we cannot of ourselves ever work our way out of sin into righteousness. But the good news is that Christ has provided the answer to our sin.

> It is a trustworthy statement, deserving full acceptance, that Christ Jesus came into the world to save sinners, among whom I am foremost *of all* (1 Tim. 1:15).

Repentance

Today there is much discussion as to the nature of saving faith as it relates to repentance. Some hold that repentance which means a change of mind, life direction, or purpose is required for salvation. While this may well be true, it often must be assumed to be part of saving faith. John clearly states the purpose of his gospel.

> ...These have been written so that you may believe that Jesus is the Christ, the Son of God; and that believing you may have life in His name (Jn. 20:31).

John speaks of “believe”, “believing”, or “believed” about 85 times yet never mentions repent or repentance even once.

Paul in his masterful treatise on the gospel in Romans only speaks of repentance one time.

> But do you suppose this, O man, when you pass judgment on those who practice such things and do the same *yourself*, that you will escape the judgment of God? Or do you think lightly of the riches of His kindness and tolerance and patience, not knowing that the **kindness of God leads you to repentance**? (Rom 2:3-4).

Elsewhere Paul uses repentance for those who have erred in their lifestyle or have not yet come to a saving knowledge of the gospel.

> I now rejoice, not that you were made sorrowful, but that you were made sorrowful to *the point of* repentance; for you were made sorrowful according to *the will of* God, so that you might not suffer loss in anything through us. For the sorrow that is according to *the will of* God produces a repentance without regret, *leading* to salvation, but the sorrow of the world produces death (2 Cor. 7:9-10).

> ...with gentleness correcting those who are in opposition, if perhaps God may grant them repentance leading to the knowledge of the truth, and they may come to their senses *and escape* from the snare of the devil, having been held captive by him to do his will (2 Tim. 2:25-26).

Near the end of his gospel Luke records some of the final instructions Jesus gave His disciples.

> Then He opened their minds to understand the Scriptures, and He said to them, "Thus it is written,

> that the Christ would suffer and rise again from the dead the third day, and that **repentance for forgiveness** of sins would be **proclaimed** in His name to all the nations, beginning from Jerusalem" (Lk. 24:45-47).

While not mentioned in John's gospel, repentance can be assumed in the act of genuine faith. For saving faith includes more than just intellectual assent to the facts of the gospel. It is a movement ***from** self-reliance **to** dependence upon the merits of Christ*. Repentance is a gift of God, it is closely associated with forgiveness and saving faith, and it can be proclaimed with the gospel.

"In Christ"

What does it mean to be "in Christ"? Is it just another way of saying that a person is a Christian? Some may understand the term this way, but I do not believe it represents the totality of the biblical usage of this term. My study leads me to believe that the three key prepositions: "into", "in", and "with" *when used in connection with Christ* often describe important relationships for the true believer.

Placed "into Christ" by the baptism of the Holy Spirit

We start with the first preposition, "into", as used in connection with Christ. The New Testament is clear that all believers are *placed* "into Christ" by the baptism of the Holy Spirit. Note carefully the following three references.

> For by one Spirit we were *all baptized into one body*, whether Jews or Greeks, whether slaves or free, and we were *all* made to drink of one Spirit" (1 Cor. 12:13).
>
> For *all* of you who were *baptized into Christ* have clothed yourselves with Christ (Gal. 3:27).
>
> Or do you not know that *all* of us who have been *baptized into Christ* Jesus have been baptized into His death? (Rom. 6:3).

In the above references "were baptized" and "were made to drink" are aorist passive in Greek meaning that our being placed "into Christ" by the Holy Spirit was done at a specific point of time in the past (if we have believed). It is not water baptism that places us "into Christ", rather, it is the work of the Holy Spirit to baptize believers "into Christ." Water baptism is the ritual entrance sign of the new covenant. Spirit baptism usually takes place before water baptism as in the case of the gentiles in the home of Cornelius.

> Surely no one can refuse the water for these to be baptized who have received the Holy Spirit just as we *did*, can he? And he ordered them to be baptized in the name of Jesus Christ (Acts 10:47-48).

Some churches insist that baptism of the Holy Spirit must be accompanied by the speaking in tongues. This was true in a few cases in the days immediately after Pentecost to give visual evidence, however, it is *not* true for Christians today, nor was it true for many in the apostolic church. *All* true believers are baptized by the Holy Spirit. Yet in 1 Corinthians 12:30, just a few verses after 12:13, listed above we read:

> All do not have gifts of healings, do they? All do *not* speak with tongues, do they? All do not interpret, do they?

We conclude, then, that the Spirit baptism happens to *all* believers who are placed "into Christ". This is the "one baptism" spoken of in Ephesians 4:5. Water baptism is the picture or symbol of Spirit baptism which takes place the instant we are incorporated "into Christ".

The important thing for us to take away from these verses is that believers are placed "into Christ" by the work of the Holy Spirit.

Placed into Christ by faith at salvation

It is true that all true believers are placed "into Christ" by the baptism of the Holy Spirit. However, the New Testament is clear that there is a response of faith that is required. The root meaning of faith in Greek is more than just belief; it includes the idea of trust. Saving faith is trusting God's work of grace *for* us.

The content of saving faith

As one reads through the Gospels it will be seen that the content or object of saving faith evolves with the progressive revelation and/or understanding of who Jesus is. For example, there are a number of incidents where it appears that the main content of faith is belief that Jesus is a healer or miracle worker. When Jesus made water into wine at Cana, Scripture states that "His disciples believed in Him".[9] True, John the Baptist had proclaimed Jesus to be "the Lamb of God", but it is evident that the disciples understanding of who Jesus is came in stages. In John chapter two we

[9] Jn. 2:11.

read that "many believed in His name, observing His signs which He was doing."[10] For the Samaritan woman at Jacob's well the content of faith was that Jesus was the coming Messiah who wanted people to worship in Spirit and in truth.[11] Today some might consider the content of this woman's faith was too minimal for salvation. However, Jesus' promise to give her the living water so that she would never thirst again seems to have been fulfilled by John's subtle statement, she "left her water pot"…. What her concept of the Messiah was is unclear. However, the record states that after Jesus stayed with the Samaritans two days, the content of saving faith was enlarged from the woman's testimony,

> He told me all the things that I *have* done (Jn. 4:39).

to,

> for we have heard for ourselves and know that this One is indeed the Savior of the world (Jn. 4:42).

In conversation with the Jews in John 8 Jesus said "before Abraham was 'I AM'", a clear reference to YHWH (Jehovah) at the burning bush.[12] The man who was born blind was healed

---

[10] Jn. 2:23.

[11] Jn. 4:24-26.

[12] Jn. 8:56-58; Ex. 3:13,14.

by Jesus with the understanding that Jesus was "a prophet".[13] Later, however, Jesus expanded the content of the healed man's faith so that he understood Jesus as "the Son of Man". Then he responded, "Lord, I believe and he worshiped Him."[14] In the final discourse after Jesus had told His disciples that He had come forth from the Father and was going back to the Father, the disciples answered,

> "Now we know that You know all things, and have no need for anyone to question You; by this we believe that You came from God." Jesus answered them, "Do you now believe?" (Jn. 16:30-31).

Prior to the cross/resurrection event the content of saving faith seems blurry at times. Nevertheless, the undergirding principle was belief and trust in the *person* of Jesus. I found it insightful that John's stated purpose in writing his gospel comes *after* his account of the resurrection and *implies* not only belief that Jesus is the Christ, but includes the belief that Jesus died for sin, was buried, and rose from the grave. John seems to define his expanded faith in his account of going to the tomb on Resurrection Sunday. He records

[13] Jn. 9:17.
[14] Jn. 9: 35-38.

how he and Peter raced to the tomb. John outran Peter; however Peter went into the tomb first. When John went in we have this poignant statement,

> So the other disciple [John] who had first come to the tomb then also entered, and ***he saw and believed***. For as yet they did not understand the Scripture, that He must rise again from the dead (Jn. 20:8-9).

Here John is saying that He believed Jesus rose from the dead when he saw the empty tomb and the grave cloths lying there, even though at that time he had no Old Testament Scripture in mind to support the resurrection.

It is after this event that he records the purpose in writing his gospel.

> Therefore many other signs Jesus also performed in the presence of the disciples, which are not written in this book; but these have been written so that you may believe that Jesus is the Christ, the Son of God; and that believing you may have life in His name (Jn. 20:30-31).

After the resurrection the content of saving faith becomes more precise. When Peter went to the home of Cornelius the points of his gospel presentation were: (1) Jesus was anointed with the Holy Spirit and with power. (2) He went about doing good and God was with Him. (3) He was put to death on a cross. (4) He rose from the dead on the third day. (5) The disciples were witnesses to all these things and they actually ate and drank with him after the resurrection. (6) He is the fulfillment of all the Old Testament prophecies. Then, (7) we have the most important gospel truth.

> Through His name everyone who believes in Him receives forgiveness of sins (Acts 10:38-43).

In the Epistles, the content of saving faith becomes even more succinct.

> That if you confess with your mouth Jesus *as* Lord, and believe in your heart that God raised Him from the dead, you will be saved; for with the heart a person believes, resulting in righteousness, and with the mouth he confesses, resulting in salvation (Rom. 10:9-10).

> Now I make known to you, brethren, the gospel which I preached to you, which also you received, in which also you stand, by which also you are saved, if you hold fast the word which I preached to you, unless you believed in vain. For I delivered to you as of first importance what I also received, that Christ died for our sins according to the Scriptures, and that He was buried, and that He was raised on the third day according to the

> Scriptures, and that He appeared to Cephas [Peter], then to the twelve (1 Cor. 15:1-5).

Here we have a well-defined four point gospel formula:

- Christ died for sin according to the Scriptures—this implies a fulfillment of all the Old Testament prophecies pointing to Christ.
- He was buried—this proves that Jesus really died.
- He was raised on the third day according to the Scriptures—this teaches us the reality of the bodily resurrection of Christ.
- He appeared (to Cephas, then to the twelve)—this tells us that there is reliable, credible eye witness evidence that Jesus really did rise from the dead.

These four points are now the content of saving faith for the Christian church. One may add to this content based upon biblical revelation,[15] however, these four points are sufficient.

---

[15] For example, Christ's deity and eternal existence, etc. which are implied in these four points.

The necessity of a faith response to the content of the gospel

When the four points of the gospel are presented,[16] the Holy Spirit is present to *give* us saving faith. Saving faith is a "gift" and it is "not of ourselves". And yet a response to the gift of faith on our part is necessary. We cannot of ourselves produce saving faith, rather it is a trustful response to the facts of the gospel generated by the Holy Spirit, yet it is required. The emphases in the following verses are mine.

> For by grace you have been saved *through faith*; and that not of yourselves, it is the gift of God (Eph. 2:8).
>
> And *without faith* it is impossible to please Him, for he who comes to God *must believe* that He is and that He is a rewarder of those who seek Him (Heb. 11:6).
>
> Jesus said to her, "Did I not say to you that *if you believe*, you will see the glory of God?" (Jn. 11:40).

---

[16] We must not limit the saving grace of God to the necessity of these four points. There are examples in Scripture and Christian experience where a person was saved without a complete understanding of these four points. However, it is clear that these are to be the content of saving faith for the Christian church.

> And *on the basis of faith* in His name, it is the name of Jesus which has strengthened this man whom you see and know; and *the faith which comes through Him* has given him this perfect health in the presence of you all (Acts 3:16).

> And Philip said, *"If you believe* with all your heart, you may." And he answered and said, *"I believe* that Jesus Christ is the Son of God" (Acts 8:37).

> ...that *if you confess* with your mouth Jesus *as* Lord, and *believe in your heart* that God raised Him from the dead, you will be saved (Rom. 10:9).

> For *if we believe* that Jesus died and rose again, even so God will bring with Him those who have fallen asleep in Jesus (1 Thess. 4:14).

> ...having been buried with Him in baptism, in which you were also raised up with Him *through faith* in the working of God, who raised Him from the dead (Col. 2:12).

While saving faith is a gift of the Holy Spirit these verses underline the necessity of a faith response to the facts of the gospel.

The prescribed order of salvation

We cannot say that the prescribed order of events is set in stone. Rather, God's great love for us draws us to Himself in various ways, nevertheless, there seems to be an approved or prescribed order that is generally true.

> In Him, you also, after listening to the message of truth, the gospel of your salvation—having also believed, you were sealed in Him with the Holy Spirit of promise (Eph. 1:13).

This important verse lists the three constituent parts of the one event of being placed into Christ by faith at salvation:

1. We hear the gospel.
2. We respond in faith—we believe and trust our life to Christ.
3. We are sealed by the Holy Spirit.

Salvation terms

There are a number of terms used for the one event when we are placed into Christ:

1. Believe in Christ
2. Baptized by the Spirit
3. Sealed by the Holy Spirit
3. Saved
4. Justified
5. Redeemed
6. Receive eternal life

Change of family

The moment we are placed "into Christ" by the baptism of the Holy Spirit we are *moved* from the fallen, condemned family of Adam into the redeemed, justified family of Christ. It is at this point that the great exchange takes place.

> For if by the transgression of the one, death reigned through the one, much more those who receive the abundance of grace and of the gift of righteousness will reign in life through the One, Jesus Christ. So then as through one transgression there resulted condemnation to all men, even so through one act of righteousness there resulted justification of life to all men. For as through the one man's disobedience the many were made sinners, even so through the obedience of the One the many will be made righteous (Rom. 5:17-19).

God has no grandchildren. No one can be saved by the faith of a parent, mentor, or anyone else. Relationship with the Risen Christ must be a personal thing. The Holy Spirit does His work when we hear the gospel and respond in faith. It is a personal work that no one can do for another. As Jesus told Nicodemus, "You *must* be born again, or born from above".[17] *There is no other way.*

Placed into Christ summary

Scripture uses many terms to represent our placement "into Christ". However, no matter what the term used, *usually* the following events happen in the order listed:

1. There is a four point gospel presentation:
    a. Christ died for our sins according to the Scriptures.
    b. He was buried.
    c. He was raised on the third day according to the Scriptures.
    d. He appeared to credible eye witnesses.
2. There is a faith response to the gospel. We believe and trust all four points of the gospel.
3. At the instant of saving faith we are placed *into* Christ by the baptism or sealing of the Holy Spirit.
4. At this same instant, we are moved from the condemned family of Adam into the justified family of Christ.
5. God has no grandchildren, only sons and daughters. One cannot rest on the faith of

[17] The Greek word ἄνωθεν can be translated either "again" or "from above".

another. One cannot trust his/her *own* theology for salvation. Being placed "into Christ" is not the same as "conversion to a system of truth". Rather there must be a personal encounter with God.

CHAPTER
Three

Justification

No book of the Bible has had a greater impact on the Christian church than the book of Romans. It was my study of this book that opened the doors wide so that the grace of God could shine through. Leon Morris, renowned New Testament scholar and author of over 50 books, said Romans 3:21-26: "...is possibly the most important single paragraph *ever written*" [anywhere, anytime].[18] Here is this section from the New American Standard Bible.

> But now apart from the Law *the* righteousness of God has been manifested, being witnessed by the Law and the Prophets, even *the* righteousness of God through faith in Jesus Christ for all those who believe; for there is no distinction; for all have sinned and fall short of the glory of God, being justified as a gift by His grace through the redemption which is in Christ Jesus; whom God displayed publicly as a propitiation in His blood

[18] Morris, *The Epistle to the Romans,* p. 173.

> through faith. *This was* to demonstrate His righteousness, because in the forbearance of God He passed over the sins previously committed; for the demonstration, *I say*, of His righteousness at the present time, that He might be just and the justifier of the one who has faith in Jesus.

It only takes about 37 seconds to read these six verses, but when we are through do we really understand what we have read? These verses carry a train load of truth which have changed the history of Christianity, sparked revivals of faith, and have been instrumental in the salvation of thousands, if not millions of people. Let's unpack their meaning.

Three metaphors are used here. But they are more than just metaphors; they expand our understanding of the gospel. **Justification** derives from the legal court system. **Redemption** comes from the world of slavery, and **propitiation** originates from the practice of sacrifice. They are the **what**, **how**, and **why** of the gospel. Together they are the fire radiating like a rainbow from the many faceted diamond of the gospel. Redemption and propitiation will be the subject of future chapters.

The first point we need to remember comes from the first two words "**But now**". These two words are used by New Testament writers to announce that a **radical change** has taken place with profound implications.[19] **But Now** gets our attention; it tells us that the new covenant changes everything—radically.

What are the profound, radical truths to which Paul refers here in our text? They come in quick succession like cars racing bumper to bumper in the Daytona 500.

> **But now apart from the Law** the righteousness of God has been manifested, being witnessed by the Law and the Prophets (Rom. 3:21).

The Jews believed there was a coming day of judgment when God would condemn and punish all who had broken His laws. That day would terminate the present world and usher in the wonderful age to come for all those whom God judged to be worthy. They held that the way to gain righteousness with God was to give alms, fast, pray, and strictly keep the law.[20] They saw God as a just God who would justify the righteous and condemn the wicked. To get the verdict of righteousness, they had to be righteous. They had

---

[19] See Jn. 15:22; Rom. 6:21-23; Rom. 7:5, 6; Rom. 11:30; 1 Cor. 15:19, 20; Gal. 3:24, 25; Eph. 5:8.

[20] Lk. 18:12; Mt. 23:23.

to have many righteous deeds to tip the balance in their favor in the judgment. Jewish life was centered on the law. As we read through the Gospels and Epistles this fact pops up time and time again. The Jews were zealous law keepers.

Paul, however, makes it clear that this radical "righteousness of God" is revealed *apart from the law*. The Greek has no definite article, so we should read "apart from law", all law, any law. This righteousness has nothing to do with law keeping. In fact, these three words, "Apart from law" exclude ***all*** human activity.[21]

This created a major problem for the Jews of Paul's day. They were so married to the law that to conceive the righteousness of the gospel was apart from law remained a stumbling block. The early Hebrew Christians fought the simple gospel as proclaimed by Paul.[22] And sad to say, there are some, perhaps many, church leaders who are still tied to law-righteousness in some form or another.

The first five words of Romans 3:21 compared with Romans 10:4 carry profound truth for those of us who grew up on law.

---

[21] Morris, *The Epistle to the Romans,* p. 171.

[22] This is demonstrated throughout the book of Acts and it is the issue in the book of Galatians.

> But now **apart from law** the righteousness of God is revealed..."
>
> For Christ is the end of the law for righteousness to everyone who believes (Rom. 10:4).

Commenting on this text, Leon Morris states,

> Romans 10:4, makes it clear that there can be no way of law for the believer. For Paul it was absolutely basic that no righteousness of human origin could avail in the sight of God.[23]

So the second section of our text is clear: God's righteousness is revealed apart from law. Romans 3:20 makes it clear.

> Because by the works of the Law no flesh will be justified in His sight; for through the Law comes the knowledge of sin.
>
> But now apart from the Law the righteousness of God has been **manifested**, being witnessed by the Law and the Prophets (Rom. 3:21).

Verse 21 when rightly interpreted deals with the **manifestation** or the **disclosure** of God's Righteousness.

Verse 22 deals with the **method of receiving** God's righteousness and the **range of its effectiveness.**

---

[23] Morris, *The Apostolic Preaching of the Cross*, p. 276.

> ...even *the* righteousness of God **through faith in Jesus Christ** for **all those who believe**; for there is no distinction (Rom 3:22).

God's righteousness is available to all who exercise their faith and no one is excluded. The gospel is available to whomever trusts Christ—His life, death, and resurrection.

It is important that we understand the difference between "the righteousness of God" and "the righteousness of the law." Especially for those who come from a law-focused religion. Probably the best reference to show this is Paul's statement in Philippians 3:8, 9.

> As to the **righteousness which is in the Law, found blameless**. But whatever things were gain to me, those things I have counted as loss for the sake of Christ. More than that, I count all things to be loss in view of the surpassing value of knowing Christ Jesus my Lord, for whom I have suffered the loss of all things, and **count them but rubbish** so that I may gain Christ, and may be found in Him, ***not*** having a righteousness of my own **derived from the Law**, but that which is through faith in Christ, **the righteousness which comes from God on the basis of faith**.

Without question this verse shows that these two types of "righteousness" can *never* be equated. New covenant righteousness is above the righteousness of the law. It is the very righteousness of God.[24]

> For all have sinned and fall short of the glory of God (Rom. 3:23).

"Have sinned" is in the aorist tense, a sin of finality. There is no changing the fact that we are sinners through and through. "Fall short" is in the present tense indicating durative, continuing action. We all *continue* to fall short of God's glory. I think what Paul means here by "glory" is similar to his use of this word in 2 Corinthians 3:18.

> But we all, with unveiled face beholding as in a mirror the glory of the Lord, are being transformed into the same image from glory to glory, just as from the Lord, the Spirit.

Here "glory" seems to be the perfection of God. If this is Paul's meaning, then Romans 3:23 could read like this: "For all have sinned and we continue to fall short of God's perfection or ideal." And this harmonizes with other Scriptures.

> If we say that we have no sin, we are deceiving ourselves, and the truth is not in us (1 Jn. 1:8).

---

[24] For more in-depth understanding of this point, see Ratzlaff, *Sabbath in Christ*, LAM Publications, LLC, Camp Verde, AZ, Chapter "A Better Law".

> ...being **justified** as a gift by His grace through the redemption which is in Christ Jesus (Rom. 3:24).

What does justification mean? It is a legal word used in court proceedings. It is the very foundation of the gospel and warrants our careful study. Justification carries two meanings: (1) declared not guilty or acquitted of *all* the charges (sin); and (2) declared or pronounced righteous with the very righteousness of God.

Justification does **not** mean to make righteous. It is necessary to be able to prove this from Scripture. Catholic theology holds that justification is God placing His righteousness *into us* and the method for doing this is through sacraments, such as participation in the Mass. Some, not all, leaders in the Seventh-day Adventist church hold a similar understanding of justification. However, for them the imparted righteousness is not achieved through involvement with the sacraments; rather it is a mixture of the work of the Holy Spirit in the believer and carefully obeying the Ten Commandments. Below are two references. One from the New American Standard Bible and one from Adventist's *The Clear Word.*[25]

> He made Him who knew no sin *to be* sin on our behalf, so that we might become the righteousness of God **in Him** (2 Cor. 5:21 NASB).
>
> For God made Christ to be sin for us, who knew no sin, so that He might **pour Christ's righteousness into us** so we could become more like God (2 Cor. 5:21 TCW).

Paul makes it very clear that the righteousness of justification is an *external* righteousness "in Christ", a phrase he uses about 85 times in his epistles. For example, in Romans 4:2-5 Paul is very clear.

> For if Abraham was justified by works, he has something to boast about, but not before God. For what does the Scripture say? "ABRAHAM BELIEVED GOD, AND IT WAS CREDITED TO HIM AS RIGHTEOUSNESS." Now to the one who works, his wage is not credited as a favor, but as what is due. But to the one who does not work, but believes in Him who **justifies the ungodly**, his faith is *credited* as righteousness (Rom. 4:2-5).

[25] Jack J. Blanco, *The Clear Word*, An Expanded Paraphrase of the Bible to Nurture Faith and Growth, Review and Herald Publishing Association, Hagerstown, MD, 1994.

In the next few verses Paul shows the second meaning of justification.

> Just as David also speaks of the blessing on the man to whom God credits righteousness apart from works: "BLESSED ARE THOSE WHOSE LAWLESS DEEDS HAVE BEEN FORGIVEN, AND WHOSE SINS HAVE BEEN COVERED" (Rom. 4:6-7).

Lest there be any misunderstanding, Paul expands the scope of those who qualify for justification to include people who are helpless, ungodly, and sinners who are enemies of God when they place their faith in Christ.[26] I remember when the force of these verses hit home to me. I said, "I can qualify! I am a helpless, ungodly sinner."

I happened to be watching TV when the verdict of the court was read to Casey Anthony. Tears came to my eyes when I realized the parallel of that verdict to the declaration of justification. Most of us believed Casey had killed her daughter, little Caylee. But when the judge said, "The court finds you not guilty." It did not matter whether or not she had done that terrible thing. The declaration of the court stands!

---

[26] Rom. 5:6, 8, 10.

The good news of the new covenant gospel is that if we have placed our faith in the life, death, and resurrection of Jesus Christ we are acquitted of all sin—our personal sin and the sin we inherited from Adam. The Supreme Court of the universe has acquitted us of all sin and has declared that we are righteous with the very righteousness of God. Don't let anyone try to take that verdict away from you! Later in Romans 8 Paul will write,

> Who will bring a charge against God's elect? God is the one who justifies (Rom. 8:33).

Justification by faith is the centerpiece of the gospel. In human terms, being justified before God is like winning the spiritual lottery. Things which we have always wanted, strived for, prayed for, and wished for, but could not achieve, are now ours for the taking. These will be referenced in following chapters. The truth will make you free. Yes, you will be free indeed!

He redeemed us while we were still helpless, ungodly sinners, even His enemies

CHAPTER
Four

REDEMPTION

This chapter continues the theme of being placed "into Christ". In the last chapter we looked at justification which takes place at the point of saving faith—when we are baptized by the Holy Spirit. At that point we are forgiven of all our sin, personal and inherited from Adam, and declared righteous with the very righteousness of God. This chapter deals with the legal issues of how God can do this and continues our study of Romans 3:21-26, considered by many scholars to be one of the most important sections of the entire Bible. We pick up in verse 24.

> Being justified as a **gift** by His **grace** through the **redemption** which is in Christ Jesus.

Justification can never be an isolated event

Paul carefully links justification with redemption and propitiation. God always acts justly so justification can never be an isolated event. One cannot just say, "You are declared righteous", period. The pronouncement of being declared righteous must rest on either one of two things: (1) it must be true that the person is righteous, or (2) there must be a legal way where justice is fully carried out in order to declare a person righteous when he is not. Redemption is one of the foundational pillars for justification.

Redemption

What does Redemption really mean? It is a metaphor from the practice of slavery.

> ...being justified as a gift by His grace through the *redemption* which is in Christ Jesus (Rom. 3:24).

Quoting now from Leon Morris,

> The actual usage of ἀπολυτρώσεως the Greek word from which we get Redemption, shows "ransoming" rather than "deliverance" to be the essential meaning of the word.[27]

Redemption includes the idea of freedom or deliverance, but the concept of ransoming is much bigger than deliverance or being "freed" as some Bibles translate this term.[28] There are at least six concepts that are carried by the idea of redemption. To illustrate these we will look at

---

[27] Morris, *The Apostolic Preaching of the Cross,* p. 41

[28] See the New Living Translation at Romans 3:24.

several Old Testament examples. Remember, Paul said that this righteousness of God was manifested apart from law, but was witnessed by the law and prophets.

1. **Redemption is for people in bondage.**

> Say, therefore, to the sons of Israel, "I am the LORD, and I will bring you out from under the **burdens** of the Egyptians, and I will deliver you from their **bondage**. I will also **redeem** you with an outstretched arm and with great judgments" (Ex. 6:6).

Redemption is for people who are in the bondage of slavery. Let's not leave this first concept too quickly. Perhaps you, the reader, may be in some kind of bondage. Is there some sin, abuse, evil habit that is eating away your soul? If so, you need a Redeemer and the good news is *you qualify for redemption!* Because redemption is for those who *cannot free themselves.* You need Christ. In Mark 2:17 we read,

> Jesus said to them, "It is not those who are healthy who need a physician, but those who are sick; I did not come to call the righteous, but sinners."

So the first concept included in redemption is that it is for slaves, sinners, people who are in bondage.

2. Redemption requires a price to be paid.

Following are a few verses from Old Testament laws that speak of redemption. Notice that a ransom price is required before redemption can take place.

> If, however, an ox was previously in the habit of goring and its owner has been warned yet he does not confine it and it kills a man or a woman, the ox shall be stoned and its owner also shall be put to death. If a **ransom** is demanded of him, then he shall give for the **redemption** of his life whatever is demanded of him (Ex. 21:29, 30).

Here we see the second idea in redemption is that a ransom price has to be paid before redemption could take place. Look again at our text in Romans 3:24.

> ...being justified as a gift by His grace **through the redemption** which is in Christ Jesus."

We read in Matthew 20:28,

> Just as the Son of Man did not come to be served, but to serve, and to give His life a *ransom* for many.

Christ Jesus is the one who paid the ransom price so that He could declare us not guilty of all our sin, and He did it in a way that satisfied divine justice.

3. Redemption carries the idea of substitution.

> Then the LORD spoke to Moses, saying, "Take the Levites *instead of* all the firstborn among the sons of Israel and the cattle of the Levites. And the Levites shall be Mine; I am the LORD. For the *ransom* of the 273 of the firstborn of the sons of Israel who are in excess beyond the Levites, you shall take five shekels apiece, per head (Num. 3:44-46).

Moses was to take the Levites "instead of" the first born. Substitution is a central theme of the gospel.

> He made Him who knew no sin to be sin on our behalf, so that we might become the righteousness of God in Him (2 Cor. 5:21).

Here we find the third concept in redemption is the idea of substitution. This concept will be expanded in a later chapter.

4. Redemption expresses a change of masters.

> Then I will take you for My people, and I will be your God; and you shall know that I am the LORD your God, who brought you out from under the burdens of the Egyptians (Ex. 6:7).

Notice what God did with Israel. They were in slavery to the Egyptians, in essence they were owned by their slave masters. Much like the slaves in our country were owned by their southern cotton growers. What God did was to redeem Israel from Egyptian bondage, but he did not just send them out into the wilderness on their own. No, He purchased them for Himself. They were now *owned* by the Lord. Redemption gives us a new owner, a change of masters. Paul emphasized this truth as applied to believers in Romans 6.

> But thanks be to God that though you were slaves of sin, you became obedient from the heart to that form of teaching to which you were committed, and *having been freed from sin, you became slaves of righteousness* (Rom. 6:17, 18).

> *But now having been freed from sin and enslaved to God,* you derive your benefit, resulting in sanctification, and the outcome, eternal life. For the wages of sin is death, but the free gift of God is eternal life in Christ Jesus our Lord (Rom. 6:22, 23).

So the fourth concept in Redemption is that we are now under a new owner, a change of masters has taken place.

5. Our Redeemer is a good Master and wants the best for us.

> Then I will take you for My people, and I will be your God; and you shall know that I am the LORD your God, who brought you out from under the burdens of the Egyptians. I will bring you to the

> land which I swore to give to Abraham, Isaac, and Jacob, and I will give it to you for a possession; I am the LORD (Ex. 6:8).

Our new Master is not like the old slave master wanting to use us for his benefit, but our Redeemer is good and He wants the best *for us*. He has our interests in mind. He paid the price for our redemption and keeps providing for us, working all things together for good. Old Testament Israel was given the Promised Land, we are promised a better country.[29] Jesus said in John 14:3,

> If I go and prepare a place for you, I will come again and receive you to Myself, that where I am, there you may be also.

In Hebrews 12:28 we read,

> Therefore, since we receive a kingdom which cannot be shaken, let us show gratitude, by which we may offer to God an acceptable service with reverence and awe.

We do not serve our new Master to gain His approval. He redeemed us while we were still helpless, ungodly sinners, even His enemies.[30] Now we serve Him out of joy, reverence, and awe

---

[29] Heb. 11:16.

[30] Rom. 5:6-12.

because of what He has *already* done for us and what He has prepared for us in the future!

Near the end of the book of Revelation, we get a glimpse of what our Good Redeemer has in mind for us.

> Then he showed me a river of the water of life, clear as crystal, coming from the throne of God and of the Lamb, in the middle of its street. On either side of the river was the tree of life, bearing twelve kinds of fruit, yielding its fruit every month; and the leaves of the tree were for the healing of the nations. There will no longer be any curse; and the throne of God and of the Lamb will be in it, and His bond-servants will serve Him; they will see His face, and His name will be on their foreheads. And there will no longer be any night; and they will not have need of the light of a lamp nor the light of the sun, because the Lord God will illumine them; and they will reign forever and ever (Rev. 22:1-5).

We see that the fifth concept in Redemption is that we have a good Redeemer, one who wants the best for us, one who has an unbelievably good inheritance waiting for us.

6. We have a "Kinsman Redeemer".

The concept of a kinsman redeemer is found in the Levitical laws. Once again we see the prophetic nature of the law as Paul said in Romans

3:21, "being witnessed by the Law and the Prophets". A kinsman redeemer is a beautiful Old Testament picture of Christ.

> Now if the means of a stranger or of a sojourner with you becomes sufficient, and a countryman of yours becomes so poor with regard to him as to sell himself to a stranger who is sojourning with you, or to the descendants of a stranger's family, then he shall have redemption right after he has been sold. One of his brothers may redeem him, or his uncle, or his uncle's son, may redeem him, or one of his blood relatives from his family may redeem him (Lev. 25:47-49).

There were four qualifications for a Kinsman Redeemer:

a. He must be a *blood relative*.

> And the Word became flesh and dwelt among us (Jn. 1:14).

Jesus took on real humanity demonstrated by the blood shed on the cross. Therefore He could serve as our Kinsman Redeemer, something an angel could not do.

b. He must Himself be *free*.

One slave could not redeem another slave. Here we see the importance of the sinless human nature of Christ.

> ...who committed no sin, nor was any deceit found in His mouth (1 Pet. 2:22).

c. He must be *able* to pay the price.

> Knowing that you were not redeemed with perishable things like silver or gold from your futile way of life inherited from your forefathers, but with precious blood, as of a lamb unblemished and spotless, the blood of Christ (1 Pet. 1:18, 19).

d. He must be *willing* to pay the price.

We get a glimpse into the passion of the cross as we contemplate Christ's prayer in the Garden of Gethsemane.

> Then He said to them, "My soul is deeply grieved, to the point of death; remain here and keep watch with Me." And He went a little beyond them, and fell on His face and prayed, saying, "My Father, if it is possible, let this cup pass from Me; yet not as I will, but as You will." And He came to the disciples and found them sleeping, and said to Peter, "So, you men could not keep watch with Me for one hour? Keep watching and praying that you may not enter into temptation; the spirit is willing, but the flesh is weak." He went away again a second time and prayed, saying, "My Father, if this cannot pass away unless I drink it, Your will be done." Again He came and found them sleeping, for their eyes were heavy. And He left them again, and went away and prayed a third time, saying the same thing once more. Then He came to the

> disciples and said to them, "Are you still sleeping and resting? Behold, the hour is at hand and the Son of Man is being betrayed into the hands of sinners" (Mt. 26:38-45).

Yes, our Kinsman Redeemer, knowing the price for our redemption, was willing to pay that price. So the sixth concept in redemption is that of a Kinsman Redeemer, a blood relative, who is free, who has the assets to pay the ransom price, and is willing to pay that price.

The redemption taught in the Bible is a beautiful thing. It is so much more than just "deliverance" or "being set free" as some of the modern translations render it. Let us read again Romans 3:24-26.

> Being justified as a gift by His grace through the redemption which is in Christ Jesus; whom God displayed publicly as a propitiation in His blood through faith. This was to demonstrate His righteousness, because in the forbearance of God He passed over the sins previously committed; for the demonstration, I say, of His righteousness at the present time, so that He would be just and the justifier of the one who has faith in Jesus (Rom. 3:24-26).

Could it be that Christ actually became an *abomination* for us suffering the wrath of God so that God could justify us poor sinners?

CHAPTER Five

PROPITIATION

In this chapter we continue our study of Romans 3:21-26. In an earlier chapter we dealt with justification—the acquittal from all sin, and the declaration of being counted righteous with the very righteousness of God. In the last chapter we studied redemption which gave one of the legal underpinnings to justification—the ransom price was paid by the blood of Christ. In this chapter we consider propitiation a second supporting pillar of justification.

> Whom God displayed publicly as a **propitiation** in His blood through faith. This was to demonstrate His righteousness, because in the forbearance of God He passed over the sins previously committed; for the demonstration, I say, of His righteousness at the present time, so that He would be just and the justifier of the one who has faith in Jesus (Rom. 3:25-26).

Propitiation is a term with which most of us are unfamiliar. It derives its meaning from the concept of sacrifice. Paul brings this term in here for good reason as there are *two additional theological problems* that must be addressed in his teaching on justification by faith.

He passed over the sins previously committed

Anyone who reads the Old Testament stories, or studies history for that matter, recognizes that sometimes the guilty seem to go free or at least just get a slap on the hand. For example, in 1 Kings 11:3-12, we read that Solomon had some 700 wives, and when he was old they turned his heart away from the Lord to serve other gods. Here is what God said to Solomon. See if you think this is justice.

> Because you have done this, and you have not kept My covenant and My statutes, which I have commanded you, I will surely tear the kingdom from you, and will give it to your servant. Nevertheless I will not do it in your days for the sake of your father David, but I will tear it out of the hand of your son.

What kind of justice is this? Paul recognized that many times God in his forbearance *passed over sins* without giving them their full due. Justice demands that all these "passed over sins" must meet their *full* penalty and that is the function of propitiation.

Justification appears to contradict Old Testament teaching.

This section of Romans is not asking how a just God can allow sinners to go to hell. Rather, the issue here is, how a just God can allow sinners to go to heaven. It is as if we are seeing the gospel from God's perspective.

The second problem addressed in this text is that there are a number of texts in the Old Testament that appear to be in *direct contradiction* to Paul's gospel of justification by faith. Consider the following:

> You shall not pervert the justice due to your needy brother in his dispute. Keep far from a false charge, and do not kill the innocent or the righteous, ***for I will not acquit the guilty*** (Ex. 23:7).

Really? Does not Paul tell us how God justifies helpless, ungodly, sinners who are enemies of God?[31] Wouldn't that qualify one as being guilty?

> If there is a dispute between men and they go to court, and the judges decide their case, and they **justify the righteous and condemn the wicked**, then it shall be if the wicked man deserves to be

[31] Rom. 5:6-10.

> beaten, the judge shall then make him lie down and be beaten in his presence (Deut. 25:1-2).

However in our passage in Romans Paul is stating that God justifies the *wicked!* Yet in the Old Testament we read differently.

> The LORD is slow to anger and abundant in lovingkindness, forgiving iniquity and transgression; but **He will by no means clear the guilty** (Num. 14: 18).

But that is exactly what justification by faith does!

> Woe to those …Who *justify the wicked* for a bribe" (Isa. 5:23).

> He who justifies the wicked and he who condemns the righteous, both of them alike are an ***abomination*** to the LORD (Prov. 17:15).

The meaning of Propitiation

Do you see the deep issues involved? The heart of the new covenant gospel is justification by faith. This means that God declares that we are not guilty when we are, and also that we are counted to have the very righteousness of God when we don't. Yet, that is exactly what God says in the Old Testament is an abomination! How do we reconcile all of this? The answer is found in the correct understanding of propitiation. What does this word mean? The Greek word group, ἱλαστήριον, has been translated as propitiation, mercy seat, sacrifice of atonement, and expiation.

All of them give slightly different shades of meaning; all of them help us understand more clearly the simple yet profound death of Christ. In the Old Testament sanctuary the mercy seat was where the high priest made atonement for the sins of Israel. Likewise it was on the cross where Christ made atonement once for all by His sacrificial death. Truly, His death was a sacrifice of atonement. The translation ἱλαστήριον as expiation[32] (the cancelation of sin) in my opinion fails to grasp the intrinsic value of what happened at the cross. It says nothing about *how* God could cancel sin. I believe propitiation includes two ideas not clearly brought out in some of the other translations of the word ἱλαστήριον. Namely, there is something done in propitiation to change the relationship between man and God, and the appeasement of God's wrath is central to that change.

Some theologians do not like the concept of God's wrath or anger; neither do they think God needs to be appeased. However, note how the

[32] See the Revised Standard Version at Rom. 3:25.

Greek word for propitiation was used in the Greek world.

> In Classical Greek…When ἱλαστήριον (propitiation) is applied to the Deity it is a means of appeasing God or averting his anger and not a single instance to the contrary occurs in the whole Greek literature.[33]

So the people to whom Romans was written would understand propitiation, not only in the Jewish idea of sacrifice of atonement from the Old Testament Scriptures, but also as ***appeasing God to avert His wrath***. Paul, in Romans 1:18-3:20 has in no uncertain terms shown that all men: gentiles, moralists, and Jews are under the wrath of God. Neither justification nor redemption deal with God's wrath, that is why Paul brings propitiation in at this point. It, like redemption, is a supporting pillar of justification. It must be shown that God has *justly* punished sin in that His wrath has been expended. God's wrath is clearly taught in Scripture. There are over a dozen Hebrew words for God's wrath and anger. It is mentioned over 500 times in the Old Testament and about 36 times throughout the New Testament.

[33] Morris, *The Apostolic Preaching of the Cross*, p. 145.

The wrath of God, however, is not God losing his temper. Rather, it is his hatred of sin. Can you imagine the sorrow, yes anger, even burning anger, that the Creator has when He sees the sin, the wars, the carnage, that are taking place in our world? We think of what went on at the Twin Towers, the murders in Libya, and what is now going on in Syria and Iraq, the videotaping of the beheading of Daniel Pearl, and dozens of Christians being crucified, burned, or buried alive by ISIS. Think of the many terrorist attacks killing innocent people in cold blood in the name of Allah. The many abductions of beautiful young girls and women who end up murdered with mutilated bodies. God's anger against sin is real. However, God's wrath can only be properly appreciated when we see it framed in His holiness.

In the **pagan** world, it was ***man*** that propitiated, or appeased the gods. However, with our God, ***<u>man has nothing to do with propitiation</u>***. Let's read our text again noting the highlighted words.

> Whom **God** displayed publicly as a propitiation in **His** blood through faith. This was to demonstrate **His** righteousness, because in the forbearance of **God He** passed over the sins previously committed;

> for the demonstration, I say, of **His** righteousness at the present time, so that **He** would be just and the justifier of the one who has faith in Jesus (Rom. 3:25, 6).

When we speak of propitiation in his blood, theologically we are gazing into the holy of holies. We remember what Isaiah said when he saw the glory of God.

> Woe is me, for I am ruined! Because I am a man of unclean lips, and I live among a people of unclean lips; for my eyes have seen the King, the LORD of hosts (Isa. 6:5).

Could it be that the holiness of God demanded complete justice? Could it be that the love of God for us poor, helpless, ungodly sinners determined that we were not going to suffer the wrath of God that we deserved; but instead *He would take that wrath upon Himself* and we would receive the verdict of acquittal and justification? On that Friday afternoon of supernatural darkness when the life blood was dripping from our Lord's hands, feet and head the wrath of God against sin was propitiated. Our Kinsman Redeemer who was our brother in the flesh, who was free from the bondage of sin, who could pay the price for our redemption, chose to do it. We sense the terrible, unspeakable agony, "My God, My God, *why* have you forsaken Me"? Could it be that Christ actually became an *abomination* for us suffering the wrath of God so that God could justify us poor sinners in a way that fully met His infinite justice?

We have been delivered from the slavery of sin and wrath. Our Redeemer is strong and good. He has purchased us for Himself and has given us a lasting inheritance. He took the wrath in our place.

> He made Him who knew no sin to be sin on our behalf, so that we might become the righteousness of God in Him (2 Cor. 5:21).
>
> Therefore, He had to be made like His brethren in all things, so that He might become a merciful and faithful high priest in things pertaining to God, to make **propitiation** for the sins of the people (Heb. 2:17).
>
> He Himself is the **propitiation** for our sins; and not for ours only, but also for those of the whole world (1 Jn. 2:2).
>
> In this is love, not that we loved God, but that He loved us and sent His Son to be the **propitiation** for our sins (1 Jn. 4:10).

As we contemplate sin, justification, redemption, and propitiation we get a sense of God's infinite holiness, justice, and love. Not only that, but considering the price paid for our redemption and the wrath of God poured out on our Substitute in propitiation **we get an expanded appreciation of our own value in the sight of God**. Paul will develop this later in his letter to Romans.

> But God demonstrates His own love toward us, in that while we were yet sinners, Christ died for us. Much more then, having now been justified by His blood, ***we shall be saved from the wrath of God through Him***. For if while we were enemies we were reconciled to God through the death of His Son, *much more,* having been reconciled, we shall be saved by His life. And not only this, but we also exult in God through our Lord Jesus Christ, through whom we have now received the reconciliation (Rom. 5:8-11).

As we contemplate the fuller meanings of justification, redemption, and propitiation we get a life-changing, blinding glimpse into the glory of the most holy place of God's being. Let's read Romans 3:25, 26 again.

> Whom God displayed publicly as propitiation in His blood through faith. This was to demonstrate His righteousness, because in the forbearance of God He passed over the sins previously committed; for the demonstration, I say, of His righteousness at the present time, so that He would be just and the justifier of the one who has faith in Jesus (Rom. 3:25-26).

The gospel is the story of a finished atonement. It tells us how a just God can legally accept sinners into his family and ultimately change them into His likeness. Wow! What a God!

Our job is to proclaim that *finished work* of Calvary to a hostile and dying world. And when we do, we have the promise that our Redeemer will come to take us to the glorious home being prepared for us![34] Romans 3:21-26 deserves to be memorized, contemplated, and accepted. When we understand this section thoroughly we may agree with Leon Morris who said this passage "is possibly the most important single paragraph *ever written*."

---

[34] "This gospel of the kingdom shall be preached in the whole world as a testimony to all the nations, and then the end will come" (Mt. 24:14). "In My Father's house are many dwelling places; if it were not so, I would have told you; for I go to prepare a place for you. If I go and prepare a place for you, I will come again and receive you to Myself, that where I am, there you may be also" (Jn. 14:2, 3).

Much more, having been reconciled, we shall be saved by His life

CHAPTER Six

Reconciliation

In this chapter we consider reconciliation, another beautiful facet of the diamond of the gospel; one act that brought two estranged parties together and established peace.

The need for reconciliation

The estrangement between man and God had its beginning in the Garden of Eden.

> When the woman saw that the tree was good for food, and that it was a delight to the eyes, and that the tree was desirable to make *one* wise, she took from its fruit and ate; and she gave also to her husband with her, and he ate. Then the eyes of both of them were opened, and they knew that they were naked; and they sewed fig leaves together and made themselves loin coverings. They heard the sound of the LORD God walking in the garden in the cool of the day, and the man and his wife hid themselves from the presence of the LORD God among the trees of the garden. Then the LORD God called to the man, and said to him, "Where are

> you?" He said, *"I heard the sound of You in the garden, and I was afraid because I was naked; so I hid myself."* And He said, "Who told you that you were naked? Have you eaten from the tree of which I commanded you not to eat?" The man said, "The woman whom You gave *to be* with me, she gave me from the tree, and I ate." Then the LORD God said to the woman, "What is this you have done?" And the woman said, "The serpent deceived me, and I ate" (Gen. 3:6-13).

In just a few short sentences we see the tragedy of sin and the resulting estrangement as Adam and Eve tried to hide from God. Almost immediately there also developed disaffection between Adam and Eve. Adam blamed Eve and in so doing in essence blamed God for giving him Eve. Eve blamed the serpent. The peace of that perfect creation quickly came to an end. We see, then, that sin initiates the need for reconciliation. This was man's act and man's alone.

Who needs to be reconciled?

That man is estranged from God is the witness of Scripture and history. Paul in Romans 1-3 builds a strong case for man's sin and rebellion. His conclusion is that none are righteous, no not one. All have sinned and continue to fall short of God's glory. Sinful man wants both to hide from God and yet also wants to find Him. No ancient culture was without some concept of god. There was both a longing to come into the presence of God and yet a deep fear of that same presence. Estrangement between man and God, man and women, and parent and child runs like an ugly smear through the pages of history.

David summarized man's condition.

> The wicked, in the haughtiness of his countenance, does not seek *Him*. All his thoughts are, "There is no God" (Ps. 10:4).

Today most of the scientific community has dismissed God. Yet those same scientists encourage our government to spend millions, if not billions, of dollars in trying to find "god". They are listening for some intelligent communication from deep, outer space, sending space vehicles to fly by distant heavenly bodies, and developing huge telescopes to search the heavens for the origin of life. Man wants to dismiss God out of his thinking, yet deep inside there is a longing to find Him.

This estrangement is the result of sin.

> Behold, the LORD'S hand is not so short that it cannot save; nor is His ear so dull that it cannot hear. But *your iniquities have made a separation between you and your God*, and your sins have

hidden *His* face from you so that He does not hear (Isa. 59:1-2).

The nations will know that the house of Israel went into exile for their iniquity because they acted treacherously against Me, and *I hid My face from them*; so I gave them into the hand of their adversaries, and all of them fell by the sword. According to their uncleanness and *according to their transgressions I dealt with them*, and *I hid My face from them* (Ez. 39:23-24).

Then they will cry out to the LORD, But He will not answer them. Instead, *He will hide His face from them* at that time *because* they have practiced evil deeds (Mic. 3:4).

There are some theologians who claim that only man needs to be reconciled to God and not God to man. Man is reconciled to God, they would say, when he understands the depth of God's love. They do not believe that anything needed to be done by God, to God, or for God in order to reconcile God to man. Only man had to change. While it is true that there is no text in Scripture that states forthrightly that God has been reconciled to man, nevertheless there are a number of statements that clearly lead us in that direction.

For many walk, of whom I often told you, and now tell you even weeping, *that they are* ***enemies***

> of the cross of Christ, whose end is destruction, whose god is *their* appetite, and *whose* glory is in their shame, who set their minds on earthly things (Phi. 3:18-19).

> And although you were formerly **alienated** and hostile in mind, engaged in evil deeds, yet He has now reconciled you in His fleshly body through death, in order to present you before Him holy and blameless and beyond reproach (Col. 1:21-22).

> The gift is not like *that which came* through the one who sinned; for on the one hand the judgment *arose* from one *transgression* resulting in **condemnation**, but on the other hand the free gift *arose* from many transgressions resulting in justification (Rom. 5:16).

The above Scriptures indicate that there was some kind of estrangement from God's point of view in that sinful man was condemned by God. Leon Morris puts it like this:

> But if man has come under condemnation so that the sentence of God is against him, then more is required than repentance if man's rightful relationship to God is to be restored. If God's attitude to sin is expressed in condemnation then God's attitude is involved in reconciliation, for reconciliation cannot come about independently of that condemnation.[35]

[35] Morris, *The Apostolic Preaching of the Cross*, p. 245.

> God was reconciling the world to Himself. We cannot say that God was reconciled by any third party. Rather He must be thought of as reconciling Himself.[36]

Who initiates reconciliation?

There is nothing that man can do to reconcile himself to God. However, the attempt to do so has been and continues to be the teaching of all *religions* save Christianity. This is attested in all the ancient writings with lists of behaviors designed to make peace between God and man. The building of temples, pyramids, and gods of wood and stone are all attempts to find God and get God to do what man wants. But if we say that God had to change in order to be reconciled to man, how can that be? God's character is perfect and unchanging.

> God's feelings toward us never needed to be changed. But God's treatment of us, God's practical relation to us—that had to change. The distinction is important, God's love never varied. But the atonement wrought by Christ means that men are no longer treated as enemies (as their sin deserves), but as friends. God has reconciled Himself.[37]

---

[36] *Ibid.*, p. 246.
[37] *Ibid.*, p. 247.

In our culture it is usually the offending person who is expected to seek out the offended person, tell them we are sorry, and do what is needed to make reconciliation. However, God, the offended person, seeks out the offender—sinful mankind—and provides what is needed to make reconciliation

> For if while we were enemies we were reconciled to God through the death of His Son, much more, having been reconciled, we shall be saved by His life (Rom. 5:10).

The ministry of reconciliation

> Therefore if anyone is in Christ, *he is* a new creature; the old things passed away; behold, new things have come. Now all *these* things are from God, who reconciled us to Himself through Christ and gave us the ministry of reconciliation, namely, that God was in Christ reconciling the world to Himself, not counting their trespasses against them, and He has committed to us the word of reconciliation. Therefore, we are ambassadors for Christ, as though God were making an appeal through us; we beg you on behalf of Christ, be reconciled to God. He made Him who knew no sin *to be* sin on our behalf, so that we might become the righteousness of God in Him (2 Cor. 5:17-21).

The ministry of reconciliation has both a vertical and horizontal dimension. We are instructed to invite fellow sinners to accept the substitutionary death of Christ for their sin that results in them being reconciled to God. At the same time we are to initiate reconciliation if we have offended someone or if someone has offended us. In either case it is *our* responsibility to initiate the reconciliation process.

> Therefore if you are presenting your offering at the altar, and there remember that your brother has something against you, leave your offering there before the altar and go; first be reconciled to your brother, and then come and present your offering (Mt. 5:23-24).

True reconciliation cannot take place unless the cause of estrangement is identified and thoroughly dealt with. It is not enough to just let bygones be bygones. This is true with God and with our fellowmen.

> It is the consistent teaching of Scripture that man could not overcome the cause of the enmity. The barrier which the sin of man had erected the wit of man could not find means to remove. But in the death of Him whom God "made sin" for man the cause of the enmity was squarely faced and removed. Therefore a complete reconciliation results, so that man turns to God in repentance

and trust, and God looks on man with favor and not in wrath.[38]

Jesus instructs us to love our enemies. This is part of the ministry of reconciliation. It was *while* we were enemies of God that He took the initiative to provide what was needed to make reconciliation. In this we are to follow His example.

Reconciliation and peace

For it was the *Father's* good pleasure for all the fullness to dwell in Him, and through Him to reconcile all things to Himself, having made peace through the blood of His cross; through Him, *I say*, whether things on earth or things in heaven. And although you were formerly alienated and hostile in mind, *engaged* in evil deeds, yet He has now reconciled you in His fleshly body through death, in order to present you before Him holy and blameless and beyond reproach (Col. 1:19-22).

Peace in the New Testament is not simply the absence of war. It is a much more positive concept, and one which, as here, may be compatible with struggle. It stands for the spiritual well-being at the highest level, a prosperity of the soul resulting from

[38] *Ibid.*, p. 249.

being in right relationship with God. God brings about this relationship by His victory over Satan.[39]

> These things I have spoken to you, so that in Me you may have peace. In the world you have tribulation, but take courage; I have overcome the world (Jn. 16:33).
>
> Therefore, having been justified by faith, we have peace with God through our Lord Jesus Christ (Rom. 5:1).

Peace *with* God is the prerequisite for the peace *of* God. Only those who have experienced reconciliation with God experience the peace of God.

In my limited experience I have found that often the peace of God becomes reality only when I have a clear conscience. If I have offended someone or been offended by someone, the peace of God seems to vanish like rain on a sandy desert in the summer heat of Arizona. However, when I take the initiative to make things right no matter who is the offender, the peace of God returns like a gentle, refreshing rain.

The ministry of reconciliation and the peace of God are joined together like two lovers walking hand in hand.

---

[39] *Ibid.*, p. 241, 242.

CHAPTER
Seven

SUBSTITUTION—HE DID IT FOR ME!

Substitution is a gospel theme that runs through the whole of Scripture, another band of color flashing from the diamond of the gospel. Perhaps one of the most insightful and prophetic events pointing to the cross that cannot be dismissed by critics is found in Genesis 22, the story of Abraham offering up Isaac in obedience to the command of God. Often higher critics say the recorded events that appear to be a fulfilment of prophecy were actually written after the event happened. However, the parallels between this prophetic event that happened some 2,000 years before Christ and what transpired when our Lord died on the cross as our Substitute are so striking that they cannot be denied. They stand embedded in the rock of history as a solid memorial proving that the Bible is trustworthy and Christ is the promised Messiah.

> Now it came about after these things, that God tested Abraham, and said to him, "Abraham!" And he said, "Here I am." He said, "Take now your son, ***your only son***, ***whom you love***, Isaac, and go to the land of Moriah, and ***offer him*** there as a burnt offering on ***one of the mountains of which I will tell you***." So Abraham rose early in the morning and saddled his donkey, and took two of his young men with him and Isaac his son; and he split wood for the burnt offering, and arose and went to the place of which God had told him. On the third day Abraham raised his eyes and saw the place from a distance. Abraham said to his young men, "Stay here with the donkey, and I and the lad will go over there; and ***we will worship and return to you***" (Gen. 22:1-5).

This event comes late in the life of Abraham. God had already blessed Him, counted his faith as righteousness, made a covenant with him and his posterity, and miraculously given him a son in his old age. Yet God wanted to test him further and in so doing God provided for us this prophetic event with insights into the gospel truth of substitution.

One can only imagine the thoughts going through Abraham's mind. The covenant God had made was to be fulfilled through Isaac.

> But My covenant I will establish with Isaac, whom Sarah will bear to you at this season next year (Gen. 17:21).

> ...for through Isaac your descendants shall be named (Gen. 21:12).

Actually, we have no record of what went on in Abraham's mind. He knew God's voice and he had learned by experience to trust God in faith. The story forces us to put ourselves into Abraham's place and feel the emotional tension.

Abraham had left his father's home to wander about in a land that was his only by promise. He had seen the provision of the miracle birth of Isaac. Now what? Was all this for naught?

We are not told how old Isaac was on this occasion. The historian Josephus states that he was twenty five.[40] A rabbi from the middle ages stated that Isaac was thirty seven years old at this time.[41] From all indications Isaac was in the peak years of his strength in that he was able to carry enough wood for a burnt offering. Abraham was about 125-137 years old and could have easily been overpowered by his son. Yet there is not a hint of a struggle.

To understand the intricacies of this story we must see them in the light of the Trinity. We can best understand this story in Genesis if we see

---

[40] Josephus, *Antiquities of the Jews*, Book 1, Chapter XIII, Paragraph 2.

[41] Https://www.google.com/?gws_rd=ssl#q=how+old+was+isaac+ when +he+was+offered+up

both Abraham and Isaac representing different facets of the Christ event as God the Father and Christ the obedient, only beloved Son, together worked out our salvation by the principle of substitution.

Abraham obeys God's command without question just as Christ obeyed the Father without question. Abraham and his men traveled for three days getting to the mountain that God showed him. It is significant that this mountain is the same as what we call Mt. Calvary, where the temple would later be built.[42] The fact that Abraham was specifically directed to ***this mountain*** shows God intended much more than just to test Abraham's faith. The prescribed details point us to the truth foreshadowed.

When Abraham left his men he said,

> Stay here with the donkey, and I and the lad will go over there; and ***we*** *will worship and* ***return*** *to you* (Gen. 22:5).

We could ask many questions here. Was this an expression of his God-given faith that somehow He *with Isaac* would return to his men? Knowing the many promises God had made to

---

[42] See Keil-Delitzsch, *Commentary on the Old Testament,* William B. Eerdmans Publishing Company, Grand Rapids, MI., p. 253.

Abraham which were all centered in Isaac, did Abraham believe that God could raise Isaac from the dead? This is the testimony of the writer of Hebrews.

> By faith Abraham, when he was tested, offered up Isaac, and he who had received the promises was offering up his only begotten *son*; *it was he* to whom it was said, "IN ISAAC YOUR DESCENDANTS SHALL BE CALLED." He considered that God is able to raise *people* even from the dead, from which he also received him back as a **type** (Heb. 11:17-19).

Returning to the Genesis story,

> Abraham took the wood of the burnt offering and laid it on Isaac his son, and he took in his hand the fire and the knife. So the two of them walked on together. Isaac spoke to Abraham his father and said, "My father!" And he said, "Here I am, my son." And he said, "Behold, the fire and the wood, but where is the lamb for the burnt offering?" Abraham said, "***God will provide for Himself the lamb for the burnt offering***, my son." So the two of them walked on together. Then they came to the place of which God had told him; and Abraham built the altar there and arranged the wood, and bound his son Isaac and laid him on the altar, on top of the wood (Gen. 22:6-9).

Abraham took the **wood** and *laid it on Isaac his son*. Then on top of the mount he bound Isaac and *laid him on the altar, on top of the **wood***. One cannot read this account without seeing this event as foreshadowing the cross of Christ.

To interpret this event as foreshadowing Christ is not wild allegorizing. Not only did the writer of Hebrews see this event as a "type", but Christ in one of His most revelatory statements, points us in this direction.

> Jesus answered, "If I glorify Myself, My glory is nothing; it is My Father who glorifies Me, of whom you say, 'He is our God'; and you have not come to know Him, but I know Him; and if I say that I do not know Him, I shall be a liar like you, but I do know Him, and keep His word. ***Your father Abraham rejoiced to see My day, and he saw it and was glad***." The Jews therefore said to Him, "You are not yet fifty years old, and have You seen Abraham?" Jesus said to them, "Truly, truly, I say to you, before Abraham was born, I am." Therefore they picked up stones to throw at Him; but Jesus hid Himself, and went out of the temple (Jn. 8:54-59).

It was here on the mountain top that Abraham clearly saw "Christ's day"—the gospel of substitution.

> And Abraham stretched out his hand, and took the knife to slay his son. But the angel of the LORD called to him from heaven, and said, "Abraham, Abraham!" And he said, "Here I am." And he said,

> "Do not stretch out your hand against the lad, and do nothing to him; for now I know that you fear God, since you have not withheld your son, your only son, from Me." Then Abraham raised his eyes and looked, and behold, behind *him* a ram caught in the thicket by his horns; and Abraham went and took the ram, and **offered him up for a burnt offering *in the place of his son*** (Gen. 22:10-13).

The facts related in this story build a monumental prophetic event. A sanctified imagination cries out for us to fill in the missing bricks in this sacred memorial. That Isaac, now a strong young man, offered no resistance is significant. In his quiet acceptance of his father's will we see a preview of Christ's submission to His Father.

> Now My soul has become troubled; and what shall I say, "Father, save Me from this hour"? But for this purpose I came to this hour (Jn. 12:27).

The next few statements complete the truth of this event.

> Abraham called the name of that place The LORD Will Provide, as it is said to this day, "In the mount of the LORD it will be provided" (Gen. 22:14).

Two thousand years before the death of Christ this prophetic event showed Abraham the meaning of the substitutionary atonement.

> He [Abraham] beholds it [Christ's day] in a threefold figure. First of all, when he takes the knife, and stretches forth his hand to slay his son, he is made to realize the intensity of the love of him who spared not his own Son, but gave him up even to the death. Again, secondly, in the ram provided for Isaac's release, there is a vivid representation of the great principle of the sacrifice of Christ—that principle of substitution. A ransom is found for the doomed and condemned—an acceptable victim is put in their place. But, thirdly and especially, in the reception of Isaac again by Abraham virtually from the dead, and his welcome restoration to his father's embrace;—not, however, without a sacrifice, not without blood;—the resurrection of the Son of God, and his return to the bosom of the Father—after really undergoing that death which Isaac underwent only in a figure—might be clearly and strikingly discerned.[43]

Today there are some theologians and teachers who want to relegate the substitutionary atonement along with shedding of blood to primitive cultures. They say that God is not interested in blood and there was no reason why Christ had to die for sin. Rather, they say, Christ died to show men that they could do whatever they wanted to Him and he would love them still.

[43] Robert S. Candlish, *Studies in Genesis*, Kregel Publications, Grand Rapids, MI, p. 1997, p. 380.

The "gospel" they would say is just understanding the love of God and knowing that God is not angry with us, and we do not have to be afraid of Him. We simply trust His loving character.

However, it seems clear to this writer that the concept of substitution is a centerpiece of the gospel. For example, one cannot read the passage in Isaiah 53 without feeling the presence of the Holy Spirit guiding us into the truth of substitution.

> Who has believed our message? And to whom has the arm of the LORD been revealed? For He grew up before Him like a tender shoot, and like a root out of parched ground; He has no *stately* form or majesty that we should look upon Him, nor appearance that we should be attracted to Him. He was despised and forsaken of men, a man of sorrows and acquainted with grief; and like one from whom men hide their face He was despised, and we did not esteem Him. Surely our griefs He Himself bore, and our sorrows He carried; yet we ourselves esteemed Him stricken, smitten of God, and afflicted. But He was pierced through for our transgressions, He was crushed for our iniquities; the chastening for our well-being *fell* upon Him, and by His scourging we are healed. All of us like sheep have gone astray, each of us has turned to his own way; but the LORD has caused the iniquity of us all to fall on Him. He was oppressed and He

> was afflicted, yet He did not open His mouth; like a lamb that is led to slaughter, and like a sheep that is silent before its shearers, so He did not open His mouth. By oppression and judgment He was taken away; and as for His generation, who considered that He was cut off out of the land of the living for the transgression of my people, to whom the stroke *was due*? His grave was assigned with wicked men, yet He was with a rich man in His death, because He had done no violence, nor was there any deceit in His mouth. But the LORD was pleased to crush Him, putting *Him* to grief; if He would render Himself *as* a guilt offering, He will see *His* offspring, He will prolong *His* days, and the good pleasure of the LORD will prosper in His hand. As a result of the anguish of His soul, He will see *it and* be satisfied; by His knowledge the Righteous One, My Servant, will justify the many, as He will bear their iniquities. Therefore, I will allot Him a portion with the great, and He will divide the booty with the strong; because He poured out Himself to death, and was numbered with the transgressors; yet He Himself bore the sin of many, and interceded for the transgressors (Isa. 53:1-12).[44]

The writers of the New Testament speak with one voice in support of the substitutionary atonement.

---

[44] For easier reading I have taken out the capital letters in the NASB text that indicate the first line of Hebrew poetry.

Paul states:

> So then as through one transgression there resulted condemnation to all men, even so through one act of righteousness there resulted justification of life to all men. For as through the one man's disobedience the many were made sinners, even so through the obedience of the One the many will be made righteous (Rom. 5:18-19).
>
> He made Him who knew no sin *to be* sin on our behalf, so that we might become the righteousness of God in Him (2 Cor. 5:21).

Peter puts it like this:

> For Christ also died for sins once for all, *the* just for *the* unjust, so that He might bring us to God, having been put to death in the flesh, but made alive in the spirit (1 Pet. 3:18).

The concept of substitution illustrated to Abraham, prophesied by Isaiah, demonstrated at the cross, and taught in the Epistles, not only teaches us about the depth of God's love, but it grabs our heart as we realize it was all done for you and for me. He suffered for our sin so that He, in His holiness could legally adopt us back into His family as beloved sons and daughters. Like Abraham, when we understand these things we "see Christ's day" and we rejoice at the good news of the gospel of substitution.

God, who gives life to the dead and calls into being that which does not exist

CHAPTER
Eight

Abraham: Prototype of Saving Faith

In the last chapter we studied the event of Abraham's willingness to offer up his beloved son. In this chapter we examine earlier periods of Abraham's life that give us major insights regarding saving faith.

Paul refers to Abraham as a prototype of saving faith. When we understand Paul's statement in the light of the Old Testament record regarding Abraham's faith, important insights will be discovered that will help us apply the many declarations made to new covenant believers. We will better comprehend how to apply "in-Christ" truths and discover the deeper meaning of the important term, "mind set".

> What then shall we say that Abraham, our forefather according to the flesh, has found? For if Abraham was justified by works, he has something to boast about, but not before God. For what does the Scripture say? "ABRAHAM BELIEVED GOD, AND IT WAS CREDITED TO HIM AS RIGHTEOUSNESS."

> Now to the one who works, his wage is not credited as a favor, but as what is due. But to the one who does not work, but believes in Him who justifies the ungodly, his faith is credited as righteousness (Rom. 4:1-5).

Paul here refers to the record found in Genesis 12 and 15. God had promised "Abram"[45] that he would be made a "great nation".[46] However, as the years went by it became apparent that Sarai[47] was barren and was unable to have a child. Then the Lord again spoke with Abram and told him "Your reward shall be very great".[48] At this point, Abram said,

> O Lord GOD, what will You give me, since I am childless, and the heir of my house is Eliezer of Damascus? Since You have given no offspring to me, one born in my house is my heir (Gen. 15:2-3).

In answer to Abram's suggestion the Lord took Abram outside and said,

> Now look toward the heavens, and count the stars, if you are able to count them. And He said to him, So shall your descendants be. Then he believed in the LORD; and He reckoned it to him as righteousness (Gen. 15:5-6).

---

[45] His birth name, "exalted father".
[46] Gen. 12:1-3.
[47] Her birth name.
[48] Gen. 15:1.

At this point we might say that Abram believed that he and Sarai could have a son and it was this belief that God counted as righteousness. However, the years kept ticking by and no son was born. Sarai proposed to Abram that her maid, Hagar, be brought into the picture and he agreed and she bore Ishmael. Now we come to the record in Genesis 17. Abram is ninety nine years old and Sarai is ninety. The Lord expands His promise to Abram.

> As for Me, behold, My covenant is with you, And you will be the father of a multitude of nations. No longer shall your name be called Abram, But your name shall be Abraham; For I will make you the father of a multitude of nations (Gen. 17:4-5).

Then we have this astounding communication:

> Then God said to Abraham, "As for Sarai your wife, you shall not call her name Sarai, but Sarah *shall be* her name. I will bless her, and indeed I will give you a son by her. Then I will bless her, and she shall be *a mother of* nations; kings of peoples will come from her" (Gen. 17:15-16).

Now we come to what has been a helpful insight for me regarding the faith of Abraham which in turn will help us define what Paul means by "mind set". This will be discussed more fully in future chapters. But here we get a deeper understanding of Abraham's faith.

> Then Abraham fell on his face and laughed, and said in his heart, "Will a child be born to a man one hundred years old? And will Sarah, who is ninety years old, bear a child?" And Abraham said to God, "Oh that Ishmael might live before Thee!" (Gen. 17:15-18).

As one reads the above reference it is hard to comprehend how this statement could be counted as faith. I could not find any evidence *in this account* that Abraham expressed *any* faith! Some say Abraham expresses his faith by his laughing. However, the fact that he said, "Oh that Ishmael might live before Thee!" rules this out. The context makes this account of Abraham's faith even worse. Note how Sarah responded to the word of the Lord.

> Then they said to him, "Where is Sarah your wife?" And he said, "Behold, in the tent." And he said, "I will surely return to you at this time next year; and behold, Sarah your wife shall have a son." And Sarah was listening at the tent door, which was behind him. Now Abraham and Sarah were old, advanced in age; Sarah was past childbearing. And Sarah laughed to herself, saying, "After I have become old, shall I have pleasure, my lord being old also?" And the Lord said to Abraham, "Why did

> Sarah laugh, saying, 'Shall I indeed bear a child, when I am so old?' "Is anything too difficult for the Lord? At the appointed time I will return to you, at this time next year, and Sarah shall have a son." Sarah denied it however, saying, "I did not laugh"; for she was afraid. And He said, "No, but you did laugh" (Gen. 18:9-15).

Not only did Abraham laugh and express *no* faith, but Sarah did the same and then told an outright lie. Further, I noted that if Sarah's laugh was a "laugh of faith" as some claim, then God would not have questioned her laugh and she would not have lied. So we must conclude at this point that both Abraham and Sarah and *no* faith in ***their*** *ability* to have a child—none, zip, zero!

With this insight we now move to Paul's use of this illustration in Romans 4.

> (As it is written, "A father of many nations have I made you") in the sight of Him whom he believed, even God, who gives life to the dead and calls into being that which does not exist" (Rom. 4:17).

What does this verse mean? This is a very insightful verse. The marginal reading in the New American Standard is, "Calls the things which do not exist as existing." The New English Translation renders it like this:

> (As it is written, "I have made you the father of many nations"). He is our father in the presence of God whom he believed—the God who makes the dead alive and summons the things that do not yet exist as though they already do (Rom. 4:17).

God gave reproductive life to the old bodies of Abraham and Sarah and called Abraham a "Father of many nations" *before* Isaac—his name means "he laughs"—was even conceived! Interestingly, after the experience recorded in Genesis 17, Scripture never again refers to Abraham as Abram. God *accounted* Abraham a father *before* he was a father and *treated* him as such and ***Abraham accepted his new name***. The multitude of nations, or even Isaac, was present *only* by God's *declaration!* Continuing now in Romans 4 as Paul unfolds the meaning of this illustration for us.

> In hope against hope he believed, in order that he might become a father of many nations, according to that which had been spoken, "So shall your descendants be." And without becoming weak in faith he contemplated his own body, now as good as dead since he was about a hundred years old, and the deadness of Sarah's womb; yet, with *respect to the promise of God*, he did not waver in unbelief, but grew strong in faith, giving glory to God, and being fully assured that what He had promised, He was able also to perform (Rom. 4:18–21).

Now, we see it! While Abraham had *no* faith in what *he* could do, he did have faith in the *promise of God,* being fully assured that what God had promised, *God was able also to perform.*

So Abraham's faith was not in any way based upon his own ability to perform, rather it was grounded *only* in *God's promise* and *God's power!* Paul now applies this truth.

> Now not for his sake only was it written that it was credited to him, but for our sake also, to whom it will be credited, as those who believe in Him who raised Jesus our Lord from the dead, *He* who was delivered over because of our transgressions, and was raised because of our justification (Rom. 4:23-25).

Now we can summarize the "faith of Abraham" that is a prototype of saving faith for true believers. It will give us further insight into Paul's term "mind set" used in Romans 8.

Summary and application of the faith of Abraham

- When God declares us righteous by faith, He changes our name from "sinnerman" or "sinnerwoman" to "saint". Throughout the Epistles, believers in Christ are *called* "saints" or holy ones. Paul even called the Corinthians with all their shortcomings "saints"!

- As God changed Abraham's name *before* he was a father, and counted him *as* a father, so God changes our name to "saint" and counts us *as* righteous *before* we are righteous when the *only* righteousness we have is the *declaration* of God.
- We express "the faith of Abraham" which is saving faith, *not* by our faith in what we can or will do. Rather, we are to react like Abraham and recognize the *utter impossibility* of our ever achieving righteousness. Yet, if God declares us righteous, we believe it based *solely* on *God's promise* and *God's power* to fulfill His own promise.
- As Abraham accepted his changed name, so we should accept ours. We are saved "saints".
- As Abraham was never again known by his old name so we should never again consider ourselves as lost sinners.
- As God considers us righteous "Even so consider yourselves to be dead to sin, but alive to God in Christ Jesus" (Rom. 6:11). We are to

see ourselves as God sees us: "saints in Christ Jesus."

Righteousness by faith is everything we need. It includes forgiveness for all sin, and it includes Christ's perfect righteousness accredited to us. It also brings the Holy Spirit into our lives.

> Now to him who is able to do immeasurably more than all we ask or imagine, according to his power that is at work within us (Eph. 3:20).

Thus Paul could say,

> I count all things to be loss in view of the surpassing value of knowing Christ Jesus my Lord, for whom I have suffered the loss of all things, and count them but rubbish in order that I may gain Christ, and may be found in Him, not having a righteousness of my own derived from *the* Law, but that which is through faith in Christ, the righteousness which *comes* from God on the basis of faith (Phil. 3:8,9).

Yes, indeed, God counts things which do not exist as existing! And therein lies our only hope. Now I realize how careful Paul had been in his choice of illustrations!

It was a discovery of the simple new covenant gospel of God's righteousness accounted to us on the basis of faith that completely changed my previous legalistic paradigm. I discovered instead of trying to live like somebody I was not, now because of God's gift in Christ imputed to me by faith, I strive to live like the kind of person God *already* declares me to be, and so can you!

CHAPTER
Nine

Representation—I Did It "In Him"

Thus far we have dealt with some of the "big words" of the gospel: righteousness, justification, redemption, propitiation, reconciliation, and substitution. Each facet flashing out a different colored light giving us added nuances of the gospel that help us better understand the great love, mercy, and grace of God in our salvation. All of these deal with imputed righteousness—the very righteousness of God credited to us who are "in Christ".

In Romans 6 through 8 Paul, without leaving the gospel, nevertheless moves the primary focus from imputed righteousness—the righteousness of Christ credited to our account—to imparted righteousness—the righteousness of Christ worked out in our lives by the agency of the Holy Spirit. He applies gospel realities to the life experience. Paul has shown that Christ is our Substitute—He did it for us. In chapter 6 he shows that Christ is our Representative—*we* did it "in Christ"; "it" being the work of Christ. Just like David's victory over the giant Goliath was Israel's victory, because David *represented* all Israel,[49] in the same way Christ's victory is our victory. If you are into sports, when your team wins you shout out, "We won"! The team's victory is counted to be your victory. Notice how Paul brings out the truth of representation in the first part of Romans 6.

> What shall *we* say then? Are *we* to continue in sin so that grace may increase? May it never be! How shall ***we*** who died to sin still live in it? Or do you not know that all of ***us*** who have been baptized into Christ Jesus have been baptized into His death? Therefore ***we*** have been buried with Him through baptism into death, so that as Christ was raised from the dead through the glory of the Father, so ***we*** too might walk in newness of life. For if ***we*** have become united with *Him* in the likeness of His death, certainly ***we*** shall also be *in the likeness* of His resurrection (Rom. 6:1-5).

Paul states that *we* were baptized into Christ's death, *we* were buried "with Him through baptism into death". *We* were also raised from the dead "in Christ". The goal of being incorporated into

---

[49] 1 Sam. 17:4-52.

Christ is "that we too might walk in newness of life." Paul continues:

> Knowing this, that ***our*** old self was crucified with *Him*, in order that ***our*** body of sin might be done away with, so that ***we*** would no longer be slaves to sin; for ***he*** who has died is freed from sin (Rom. 6:6-7).

Look carefully at the above text. In context who died? Was it Christ or was it believers—you and me? The context application is that our "old self" (often called the "flesh") was crucified ***with*** Christ. "Was crucified", is aorist passive meaning it happened at a point of time and it was God's work, not ours. But there is more good news! We no longer are slaves to sin! For we who died "with Christ" have been "freed from sin"—perfect passive. This Greek tense tells us that we were freed from sin at a point in time and the "free-from-sin" condition remains. We live in the ongoing state of freedom from sin! Read it again!

Some of us will immediately start to argue with Paul. "Paul, that is not true in my life. I still fall short of God's ideal." But freedom from your sin and mine is God's work. Remember this statement is perfect ***passive***. Christ did it for us and we did it "in Him".

I believe that every Christian wants to be more holy, more obedient, and have more of the fruit of good works flowing from his/her life.[50] We may disagree, however, on two points: First, is the righteousness of sanctification (personal righteousness) part of the believer's right standing before God? Some teach that the gospel not only includes justification by faith, but it ***also*** includes the personal righteousness of sanctification. This, I believe is a counterfeit gospel. The first chapters of this book have given more than sufficient evidence to show that the saving gospel is God's work of grace "for us" which ***results*** in God's work of grace "in us", but that internal righteousness is **never** the basis for our right standing with God.

Second, sometimes discipleship seems to leave faith and grace behind and moves in the direction of prescribed works. Just what these works are varies from one discipler to another. Too often the focus is taken off Christ and placed back on personal behavior. "Now that you are a Christian, don't you think you should quit smoking? And did you know that Christians should not get drunk? In fact, it would be best if you were a teetotaler. The

---

[50] If this is not your desire then you need to go back to chapter 2 and pray that God will give you repentance and saving faith.

Bible teaches tithing; therefore you should start paying a tenth of your income to the church. You should also control your temper and keep your kids under control". Many disciplers promote some version of the Christian disciplines such as fasting, silence, meditation, Bible reading, witnessing, service, Bible memorization, and the list goes on.

Most of these things are or may be good. The problem comes when we begin to measure our spiritual growth by ***our*** overcoming and ***our*** performance of these activities. There is a tendency to move from the "done of the gospel", to the "do, or don't do" of these disciplines. Often discouragement comes in and shuts down Christian growth, the very thing these discipleship programs were designed to foster.

Acceptance before God does not depend on personal righteousness.

Paul's teaching in the Epistles has been a real help to me, especially the book of Romans. One day when studying Romans 6:11 I found that this verse was the ***first verse*** in Romans where the reader was told to do something. Previous to this Paul had given a thorough foundation for the need of the gospel and the theological underpinning of the gospel—God's work in Christ for us. Up to this point in Romans he has discussed: gentiles, moralists, Jews, wrath, sin, law, a righteousness apart from law, justification, redemption, propitiation, the Old Testament witness to justification by faith through the examples of Abraham and David, the results of justification, reconciliation, a comparison of Adam and Christ, and substitution.

The Path to Holiness

Chapters 6-8 describe the path to holiness and it is a "gospel path", not a "works path". It is a "grace path" not a "law path", it is a "Spirit path" not a "flesh path". All this springs from our being incorporated "in" or "with" Christ and understanding what it means for Christ to be our Representative.

Remember the faith of Abraham. His faith and trust were focused on ***God's promise*** and ***God's power*** to fulfill His own promise. He had no faith in his ability to fulfill God's promise. So it is for those of us who follow the faith of Abraham. We accept God's word, even when He says that we live in the ongoing state of freedom from sin!

> Now if we have died with Christ, we believe that we shall also live with Him, knowing that Christ, having been raised from the dead, is never

> to die again; death no longer is master over Him. For the death that He died, He died to sin once for all; but the life that He lives, He lives to God (Rom. 6:8-10).

In verse 11, as mentioned before, we come to the first admonition or instruction in the book of Romans and what is it?

> Even so consider yourselves to be dead to sin, but alive to God in Christ Jesus.

Justification is God's acquittal of all the sin we have done, are doing, or will do, and sanctification—the path to holiness—is believing what God has declared about the person who is "in Christ". **We are to see ourselves as God declares us to be**. "In Christ" we are free from sin. So the first step down the *right* path to holiness is to consider ourselves to be dead to sin. This truth is worth another read.

> Even so consider yourselves to be dead to sin, but alive to God in Christ Jesus (Rom. 6:11).

Paul admonishes us to "present yourselves to God as those alive from the dead"[51] and then in the next verse he says:

[51] Rom. 6:13.

> For sin shall not be master over you, for you are not under law but under grace (Rom. 6:14).

There are many well intentioned teachers, and I used to be one of them, who will immediately add to what Paul has just said. They will reword the above to "…you are not under the *condemnation* of the law, but the law stills serves as a guide to measure Christian living."

In other words many disciplers would say that the path to holiness is by following the law which is to regulate Christian behavior. But this is ***not*** Paul's path to holiness.

> Having been freed from sin, you became slaves of righteousness (Rom. 6:18).

Both verbs "having been freed…" and "you became…" are aorist **passive.** This indicates that these events happened at the very moment of saving faith and it was God's work that freed us from sin and made us slaves of righteousness

Romans 6 ends with,

> The wages of sin is death, but the ***free gift*** of God is eternal life in Christ Jesus our Lord (Rom. 6:23).

Wages are earned. A gift is not. Paul feels that it is so important to know that eternal life is free that he is redundant—"free gift". Perhaps someone might feel they could earn a gift, or that the gift was not totally free. The only gift I could think of that would not be free would be something like a wife buying a Christmas present for her husband, but using his credit card for the purchase! Paul on many occasions is redundant when it comes to the freeness of the gospel. He wants to drive home his "free-gift" theology.

We come now to several major insights regarding the path to holiness springing from the truth of representation. In Romans 7:1-3 Paul tells how a person is free to marry another person if his/her spouse dies. Then Paul applies this illustration.

> Therefore, my brethren, you also were made to die to the Law through the body of Christ, so that you might be joined to another, to Him who was raised from the dead, in order that we might bear fruit for God (Rom 7:4).

In Romans 6 Paul showed that ***we*** were crucified, ***we*** died, ***we*** were buried, and raised to newness of life in Christ. Thus ***we*** are free from sin and ***we*** are to consider ourselves free from sin. Now in these verses Paul states that ***we*** were made to die to the law through the [dead] body of Christ, so that ***we*** might be joined to the resurrected Christ "that ***we*** might bear fruit for God." Underline in your thinking what Paul has just said. **We bear fruit for God when our relationship with the law is *ended.*** That happened when ***we*** were incorporated with Christ in his death. Paul explains why the law is not to be the focus of the Christian's attention.

> For while we were in the flesh, the sinful passions, **which were *aroused* by the Law**, were at work in the members of our body **to bear fruit for death** (Rom. 7:4-5).

We must not leave this verse without a full understanding of what it says and does not say. Does this verse teach that focusing on the law is the path to victory and holiness? No, rather what it says is that our sinful passions are ***aroused*** by the law and these sinful passions **bear fruit for death**—the wrong path to holiness. The next verse gives the ***right path*** to holiness". Remember the words, "but now", are to tell us that a major change has taken place.

> **But now** we have been released from the Law, having died to that by which we were bound, so **that we serve in newness of the Spirit and not in oldness of the letter** (Rom. 7:6).

There can be no misunderstanding of what Paul means here. We are released from the law as a method to achieve holiness. That is the consistent teaching of Paul.

Because by the works of the Law no flesh will be justified in His sight; for through the Law *comes* the knowledge of sin (Rom. 3:20).

But now apart from the Law *the* righteousness of God has been manifested (Rom. 3:21).

For we maintain that a man is justified by faith apart from works of the Law (Rom. 3:28).

For if those who are of the Law are heirs, faith is made void and the promise is nullified; for the Law brings about wrath, but where there is no law, there also is no violation (Rom. 4:14-15).

But before faith came, we were kept in custody under the law, being shut up to the faith which was later to be revealed (Gal. 3:23).

The sting of death is sin, and the power of sin is the law (1 Cor. 15:56).

The Law came in so that the transgression would increase; but where sin increased, grace abounded all the more (Rom. 5:20).

For sin shall not be master over you, for you are not under law but under grace (Rom. 6:14).

For Christ is the end of the law for righteousness to everyone who believes (Rom. 10:4).

Romans 7:5-6 are key verses in finding the right path to holiness. These two verses serve as ***outline headings*** for the next two sections of this letter to the Romans.

> For while we were in the flesh, the sinful passions, which were *aroused* by the Law, were at work in the members of our body to bear fruit for death (Rom. 7:5).

Romans 7:5 is illustrated in Romans 7:14-25. If we focus on our personal behavior as a means of achieving holiness, our attention will not be on Christ seated at the Father's right hand. Rather, our focus will be on ***our own behavior evaluated by the law.***

We are not saying that God's moral principles no longer apply. God's eternal moral principles interpreted by the Spirit to the circumstances of life continue to have a function in the Christian life. They are imbedded in our conscience and therefore serve to (1) stop us from doing wrong, (2) prompt us in evaluating truth and error, and (3) urge us to do what is right. The important point for most of us who grew up on law is that we never measure our acceptance with God **based upon our *personal behavior* as measured by the law**. Scripture is clear that this side of the second coming **we will always fall short of God's ideal.**

When we read Romans 7:14-25 we will note that Paul uses "I" about 23 times. He uses "law" and "sin" a number of times and the "Spirit" is not even mentioned once. There is no victory in this section. Rather, Paul states that he is "sold into bondage to sin"; "I do the very thing I hate"; "sin dwells in me"; "I practice the very evil that I do not want"; I am "a prisoner of the law of sin". He ends this section with this cry.

> Wretched man that I am! Who will set me free from the body of this death? Thanks be to God through Jesus Christ our Lord! So then, on the one hand I myself with my mind am serving the law of God, but on the other, with my flesh the law of sin (Rom. 7:24-25).

This method of grappling with the sinful nature which all Christians still have is an illustration of what Paul said earlier.

> For while we were in the flesh, the sinful passions, **which were <u>*aroused*</u> <u>by the Law</u>**, were at work in the members of our body **to bear fruit for death** (Rom. 7:4-5).

Scholars have interpreted Romans 7:14-25 a number of ways. Some believe Paul is expressing his pre-Christian life. However, he uses present tense verbs in referring to his experience. Others understand this section to be a description of the conflict between our two natures: our sin nature from Adam and our new spirit nature in Christ. While this is certainly true, it does not totally solve the problem of the apparent contradiction of what Paul has just taught in Romans 3-6 as well as in his other epistles. He has just proved that in Christ we died to sin and are free from sin.[52]

I personally believe Paul is illustrating what the results will be ***if*** one chooses a "path to holiness" that is based on **personal attempts to measure up to all the dictates of the law.**

This will be the experience of a Christian who takes his focus off Christ, who does not understand representation, and "in" or "with" Christ truth, and is working on self-discipline and forced obedience.

Romans 7:6 is the key verse for the ***right path*** to holiness. This truth is repeated in Paul's epistles several times.

> But now we have been released from the Law, having died to that by which we were bound, so that we **serve in newness of the Spirit and *not* in oldness of the letter** (Rom. 7:5-6).

> Now that faith has come, we are **no longer under the supervision of the law** (Gal. 3:25 NIV).

> **But if you are led by the Spirit, you are not under the Law** (Gal. 5:18).

[52] See Rom. 6:1-7.

This truth will be illustrated in Romans 8. Paul has now shown that the path to holiness is *not* the path of the law for law only ***arouses sin***. In Romans 8, Paul immediately moves to "in-Christ" truth. He shows that this is the valid path to holiness which becomes evident in the first few verses.

> Therefore there is **now** no condemnation ***for those who are in Christ Jesus***. For the law of the Spirit of life in Christ Jesus has **set you free from the law of sin and of death**. For what **the Law could not do**, weak as it was through the flesh, God *did*: sending His own Son in the likeness of sinful flesh and *as an offering* for sin, He condemned sin in the flesh, so that **the requirement of the Law might be fulfilled in us**, who do not walk according to the flesh but according to the Spirit (Rom. 8:1-4).

Here we see a sharp contrast to Romans 7:14-25. Instead of defeat, there is immediate victory. Our eyes are removed from our own behavior and are focused on the victory Christ has *already gained* for us. And if we are "in Christ" His victory is ours because He is our Representative. The law can no longer condemn, even if we fall into temptation and sin because the law's ability to condemn stopped at the tomb. Paul has previously shown that ***we*** were crucified with Christ and ***we*** were buried with him. When we forget this and start seeking victory over sin by way of the law, it will be failure. When we move our focus away from our behavior to our position “in Christ” at the Father’s right hand, the result is that,

> **The requirement of the Law might be fulfilled in us**, who do not walk according to the flesh but according to the Spirit (Rom. 8:1-4).

This is real “gospel transformation.” Here we find a great paradox. Those who set out to live a life of holiness by careful discipline, measuring their behavior by the dictates of the law, fail to keep the law, and often become discouraged. Sometimes they pull down the standard of holiness to their level or become perfectionistic, proud, and judgmental.

On the other hand those who understand and apply “in-Christ” truth and set their mind on the many declarations made to believers and walk according to the Spirit, achieve a measure of personal holiness—obedience to God’s moral principles.

Those who focus on their own personal behavior trying to measure up to the dictates of the law are very much like the Jews of Paul’s day. While the context is different, the theology is the same.

> What shall we say then? That Gentiles, who did not pursue righteousness, attained righteousness, even the righteousness which is by faith; but Israel, pursuing a law of righteousness, did not arrive at *that* law. Why? Because *they did* not *pursue it* by faith, but as though *it were* by works. They stumbled over the stumbling stone, just as it is written, "BEHOLD, I LAY IN ZION A STONE OF STUMBLING AND A ROCK OF OFFENSE, AND HE WHO BELIEVES IN HIM WILL NOT BE DISAPPOINTED" (Rom. 9:30-33).

Many law-focused people are afraid to look away from their own behavior. They say they are justified by faith, but then, they immediately want to be sanctified (made holy) by keeping the law. The law was not designed to make one holy. Rather the law was designed to arouse and point out sin.

> For not knowing about God's righteousness and seeking to establish their own, they did not subject themselves to the righteousness of God. **For Christ is the end of the law for righteousness to everyone who believes** (Rom. 10:3-4).

I have often said that when the gospel is presented in its clarity there is room for misunderstanding. And that is the case here. Some might assume that there is nothing we have to do in sanctification other than know who we are “in Christ”. However, in sanctification there is cooperation between the work of the Holy Spirit and our own will. This will be addressed in future chapters.

CHAPTER
Ten

KNOW WHERE YOU ARE

In the last chapter we saw that Christ is our Representative. His victory is our victory. We saw that there are two main suggested "paths to holiness" by those who disciple Christians. One is to have believers begin to observe carefully their conduct and measure their spiritual progress by the law. We saw that this, while it may develop a type of forced holiness, will often lead to spiritual failure, discouragement, and defeat. For those who can muster strong discipline, it often leads to legalism, self-righteousness, and pride.

The second path is to know who we are "in" or "with" Christ and to know that we have died with Christ to the law and the law no longer has any negative claim on us.[53] Its claim on us ended in the tomb when ***we*** were buried "with Christ". Now,

[53] The new covenant law of Christ continues to have a positive function in the Christian life. It still points out sin and gives us the perfect standard of love.

we serve God "in the newness of the Spirit and not in the oldness of the letter." Following the path of the Spirit actually achieves a certain degree of righteousness *in us* to the moral principles of Scripture.[54]

When we are placed "into Christ" by the Holy Spirit there is a spiritual *movement* that takes place that has profound implications. We need to understand our *new position* "in Christ" so that we may actuate the many blessings that come from this new position. The moment we are placed "into Christ" by the work of the Holy Spirit, Christ, through the Holy Spirit, is placed "into us". This mutual indwelling promised by Christ in John 17 is now possible. The Holy Spirit will now begin the work of sanctification—changing us from our sinful ways into obedient sons and daughters of God.

> For by grace you have been saved through faith; and that not of yourselves, it is the gift of God; not as a result of works, so that no one may boast. For we are **His workmanship**, created in Christ Jesus for good works, which God prepared

[54] So that the requirement of the Law might be fulfilled in us, who do not walk according to the flesh but according to the Spirit (Rom. 8:4).

beforehand so that we would walk in them (Eph. 2:8-10).

Before we can fully understand our new position "in Christ" it is necessary to understand where Christ is and the implications that flow from *His position.*

Christ is seated at the Father's right hand

During Jesus' trail, in answer to questions if He was the Christ, He said,

But from now on THE SON OF MAN WILL BE SEATED AT THE RIGHT HAND of the power of God (Lk. 22:69).

His answer reflects Psalm 110:1.

The LORD says to my Lord: "Sit at My right hand until I make Your enemies a footstool for Your feet."

In Ephesians 1:18-23 Paul expresses the deep desire that we might fully understand what it means ***to us*** to know that the Father has seated Christ at His right hand, the position of power.

I pray that the eyes of your heart may be enlightened, so that you will know what is the hope of His calling, what are the riches of the glory of His inheritance in the saints, and what is the surpassing greatness of His power toward us who believe. *These are* in accordance with the working

> of the strength of His might which He brought about in Christ, when He raised Him from the dead and seated Him at His right hand in the heavenly *places*, far above all rule and authority and power and dominion, and every name that is named, not only in this age but also in the one to come. And He put all things in subjection under His feet, and gave Him as head over all things to the church, which is His body, the fullness of Him who fills all in all (Eph. 1:18-23).

Let us itemize why Paul feels it is so important for us to know that Christ is seated at the Father's right hand.

The eyes of your heart have been enlightened, so that:

1. ...you will know what is the **hope** of His calling, the future blessings that are now ours "In Christ".
2. ...what is the **wealth** of his glorious inheritance in the saints. Christ was glorified at the cross when he sank to the bottom of humility to reflect the great grace and love of the Father. We are glorified when in good times and bad, even in the most humiliating circumstances, we reflect the love of Christ to others.
3. ...what is the **surpassing greatness of His power toward us** who believe. Paul wants us to understand the surpassing greatness of the Father's power toward us. He would not urge this

if it were not the case that some, perhaps many, believers did not understand this. There is a good likelihood that many of us today do not comprehend the greatness of the Father's power toward us.

It is vital that we recognize that Christ is seated at the Father's right hand, the position of power, and that He is above all rule, authority, power, and dominion. The Father's right hand is the command center for the Christian life. It is the source of all spiritual power. ***The Father's right hand is to be the focus of our attention.***

Our position "in" and "with" Christ

A few verses later in his letter to the Ephesians Paul gives us an amazing insight.

> And you were dead in your trespasses and sins, in which you formerly walked according to the course of this world, according to the prince of the power of the air, of the spirit that is now working in the sons of disobedience. Among them we too all formerly lived in the lusts of our flesh, indulging the desires of the flesh and of the mind, and were by nature children of wrath, even as the rest. But God, being rich in mercy, because of His great love with which He loved us, **even when we were dead in our transgressions**, made us alive together with Christ (by grace you have been saved), **and raised us up with Him, and seated *us* with Him in the**

> **heavenly *places* in Christ Jesus, so that in the ages to come He might show the surpassing riches of His grace in kindness toward *us* in Christ Jesus** (Eph. 2:1-7).

Here Paul has in view the expanded truth of the resurrection. It was at that time that Christ was raised up and seated with the Father. If we have been placed into Christ, then it can be said that we too, were raised up with Christ and seated with Him in heaven. If we are to realize all the blessings in the relationship of mutual indwelling recorded in John 14-17 there are two concepts that we must understand. First, we must discover how these spiritual blessings are actualized. In other words, if these blessings are now "in" or "with" Christ at the Father's right hand waiting for us, what must *we* do to realize them?

Second, we need to discover what blessings are ours that are associated with our being seated "with Christ" at the Father's right hand. For example, when people receive their earthly inheritance, the first thing they want do is to read the last will and testament to see what is willed to them and then take inventory. Only then will they be able to access the full inheritance.

Set your mind on things above

We now turn to the key text for understanding how to apply "in Christ" truths to our lives.

> Therefore if you have been raised up with Christ, **keep seeking the things above**, where Christ is, seated at the right hand of God. **Set your mind on the things above**, not on the things that are on earth. For you have died and your life is hidden with Christ in God. When Christ, who is our life, is revealed, then you also will be revealed with Him in glory (Col. 3:1-4).

An understanding of the above reference is essential for accessing all of the "in" and "with" Christ truths that will be enumerated in this and the following chapter. The first thing we must *know* is that *we have been raised up with Christ*. The verb is aorist passive. This event took place at the instant we were placed "into Christ" by the baptism of the Holy Spirit, the moment of saving faith. This was purely an act of God's grace in accordance with His mercy and love.

Next, we are to "keep seeking"—an ongoing, continuing activity. But what are we to seek? Answer: "the things above, where Christ is, seated at the right hand of God." The "things" above are neuter in Greek which tells us these "things" are not persons. Therefore, these things cannot refer to the Godhead otherwise they would be rendered in the masculine gender.

These "things" are situated where Christ is, at the right hand of the Father *and that is where we are!*[55] We "have died with Christ and our life is hidden with Christ in God." This leads us to conclude that the "things" we are to "keep seeking" **are the blessings that are ours "in" and "with" Christ. We are to set our mind on these things** and not on things that are on the earth.

> And put on the **new self**, which in *the likeness of* God has been created in righteousness and holiness of the truth. Therefore, laying aside falsehood, SPEAK TRUTH EACH ONE *of you* WITH HIS NEIGHBOR, for we are members of one another (Eph. 4:24-25).

The apostle Peter using different terminology teaches the same truth.

> Grace and peace be multiplied to you in the knowledge of God and of Jesus our Lord; seeing that His divine power has granted to us **everything pertaining to life and godliness**, through the true knowledge of Him who called us by His own glory and excellence. For by these He has granted to us **His precious and magnificent promises**, so that by **them** you may become partakers of *the* divine

[55] Eph. 2:6.

> nature, having escaped the corruption that is in the world by lust (2 Pet. 1:2-4).

Peter states that God's divine power has granted to us *everything* pertaining to life and godliness. How do we actuate these gifts? We do this by applying "His precious and magnificent promises." The result, according to Peter, is that we actually become partakers of the divine nature, having escaped the corruption that is in the world by lust.

By focusing on "in Christ" truths and the precious and magnificent promises made to believers, we are changed into Christ's likeness.

Abraham became a prototype of saving faith when he believed God, not on the basis of his own ability to perform, but on God's power to fulfill His own promise. ***He believed what God declared.*** As we saw in Romans 4, Paul applied this concept to the believer. In other words, the things above where Christ is, seated at the right hand of the Father, are the many "in Christ" blessings. As God sees us in Christ, **these "in Christ" truths are *present realities* to the Father**. Just as Abraham believed God's declaration that he would be a father of a multitude of nations, so we are to believe the many "in Christ" truths and precious and magnificent promises of God's word.

Abraham's productive faith was based solely upon God's promise and God's power. He had no faith that He and Sarah could perform. It was impossible from his perspective. In the same way, we are to accept God's word and believe His declaration about the "in" and "with" Christ truths. Transforming faith brings the future into the present. So when we read about receiving "every spiritual blessing", we set our mind on the ***present reality*** that we are seated in heaven "in Christ" at the Father's right hand and have ***already*** received "every spiritual blessing".

> In other words, the believer is to take his frame of mind and to fill it with reflection on what he is and has in Christ. Not only is it a cognitive process but in Colossians 3:2 it involves the assurance that the heavenly things thought about will be the means of gaining victory over the sin nature.[56]

In Colossians the stream of Paul's thought moves from "the hope laid up for you" in heaven to the completeness we have in Christ.[57] Then he speaks about religious practices involving food, drink, festivals, new moons, and Sabbath days, as well as the worship of angels, and visions which undermine one's complete standing in Christ.

[56] Spurbeck, p. 17.

[57] "In Him you have been made complete" (Col. 2:10).

These, he states, "are of no value against fleshly indulgence."[58]

Sandwiched between the legalistic religious practices mentioned above which don't work in controlling the sinful nature, we find the key text on accessing the "in Christ" truths mentioned above in Colossians 3:1-4. Here we are told to keep seeking the things above at the right hand of God. Then immediately after this important section the thought moves to a segment describing personal victory over evil desires.

> Therefore consider the members of your earthly body as dead to immorality, impurity, passion, evil desire, and greed, which amounts to idolatry (Col. 3:5).

After this list of sins, he says,

> ...and in them you also once walked, when you were living in them. **But now** you also, put them all aside: anger, wrath, malice, slander, and abusive speech from your mouth (Col. 3:7-8).

Paul urges his readers to understand gospel transformation.

> ...lay aside the old self, which is being corrupted in accordance with the lusts of deceit, and that you be renewed in the spirit of your **mind**, and put on

[58] Col. 2:23.

> the ***new self***, which in *the likeness of* God has been created in righteousness and holiness of the truth (Eph. 4:22-24).

We find the same order in Peter's teaching. After he mentions the importance of God's precious and magnificent promises that bring to us *everything pertaining to life and godliness*, only then does he admonish us in personal holiness.

> Now for this very reason also, applying all diligence, in your faith supply moral excellence, and in *your* moral excellence, knowledge, and in *your* knowledge, self-control, and in *your* self-control, perseverance, and in *your* perseverance, godliness, and in *your* godliness, brotherly kindness, and in *your* brotherly kindness, love. For if these *qualities* are yours and are increasing, they render you neither useless nor unfruitful in the true knowledge of our Lord Jesus Christ (2 Pet. 1:5-8).

If we do not have this experience in life Peter makes it clear what is wrong.

> For he who lacks these *qualities* is blind *or* short-sighted, having forgotten *his* purification from his former sins (2 Pet. 1:9).

When we forget what God has done *for us*, then God's power to work *in us* is muted.

Personal sanctification comes after we consider the members of our earthly body as dead. We do this by "playing" in our position "in" and "with" Christ.

For example, in football each player is assigned a position in which he is to play. Success for the team comes only if every player understands his position and plays in that position. In the same way we as Christians must understand that our positon is "in" and "with" Christ at the Father's right hand. Then if we "play"—focus our attention on the "in" and "with" Christ truths and the precious and magnificent promises—we will experience the mutual indwelling promised by Christ in John 14-17.

Blessings of being "in" and "with" Christ

Most of us have never and will never win a multi-million dollar lottery. The odds are against us. That is why I don't play. However, in the spiritual realm there are no odds. We have won! The foundational blessing we referenced above in Ephesians 2:1-7 is that we are seated with Christ in heaven at the Father's right hand. That is our position and from that position flows a multitude of benefits.

At this point we will consider **one** of the many positional blessings of being "in Christ", then we will review how to access this and other blessings.

In the next chapter we will explore many other positional blessings, present possessions, and declarations of the precious and magnificent promises made to believers as our Father shows us the surpassing riches of His grace in kindness toward us "in Christ Jesus".

Every spiritual blessing

> Blessed *be* the God and Father of our Lord Jesus Christ, who has blessed us with *every spiritual blessing* in the heavenly *places* in Christ (Eph. 1:3).

"Has blessed" is in the aorist tense indicating it was done at a point in time—for us it was the instant we were placed "into Christ"! This is news that is almost too big and too good to be comprehended! *We*—this means you and I—have been blessed with *every spiritual blessing "in Christ"*. These blessings are for "us" and are ***only*** for those who have been placed "into Christ".

What are these spiritual blessings? The context of Ephesians tells us that they are found "in Christ", have their origin with the Father and are mediated to us by the Holy Spirit. Specifically they include, but are not limited to the following:

- We are chosen "in Christ"—God desires us to be His (v. 4).

- God's purpose for us is that we would be holy and blameless—His purpose *will be* fulfilled (v.4).
- We are predestined to be adopted as sons (and daughters)—we are *now* members of the heavenly family (v.5).
- We now have redemption—*the price has been paid* which set us free from the bondage of sin and the condemned family of Adam (v.7).
- We *have forgiveness of sins*—based upon the riches of the Father's grace which he lavished upon us (v.7).
- In wisdom and insight the Father has made known to us the mystery of His will—we know the plans which He has for us "in Christ" (v.9).
- We have acquired our inheritance—not something we earned, but because our Father willed it so (v. 11).
- We are sealed by the Holy Spirit—the personal guarantee of our inheritance (v. 13).
- We are now God's own possession (v.14)!

How to set your mind on things above

We receive these blessings as we set our mind on things above.

> In Colossians 3:2 the term used is a mental term. Translations that include "mind" in their text are only partially right in their translation. In the New Testament there are two roots that describe the action of the mind. These roots occur in a wide variety of forms. One involves the use of the mind in taking experience and making its knowledge a part of the mind and memory. The other term describes the activity of the mind by which it processes information and by which it uses the processed information. Some call this intuitive thinking. A better description of the meaning is that it involves the reflection of the mind on the data with which it has to work. It is the thinking process that takes a thought and evaluates it from every angle by bouncing it around in the brain attempting to consider it from every aspect…In other words, the believer is to take his frame of mind and to fill it with reflection on what he is and has in Christ. Not only is it a cognitive process but in Colossians 3:2 it involves the assurance that the heavenly things thought about will be the means of gaining victory over the sin nature. [cf. context].

> Grammar requires that reflective thinking is to be the habitual activity for the believer.[59]

We have only scratched the surface of the many "in" and "with" Christ truths and gospel declarations. These will be developed in the next chapter. However, now is the time to make these blessings our own. Go back, read the bulleted points again, meditate upon these truths. Read Ephesians 1 in your Bible. Believe what God has declared. As we do this the Holy Spirit will work out in our lives the fruit of the Spirit. He is assigned the task of taking from Christ and delivering these blessings to us.

> But when He, the Spirit of truth, comes, He will guide you into all the truth; for He will not speak on His own initiative, but whatever He hears, He will speak; and He will disclose to you what is to come. He will glorify Me, for He will take of Mine and will disclose *it* to you. All things that the Father has are Mine; therefore I said that He takes of Mine and will disclose it to you (Jn. 16:13-15).

---

[59] Spurbeck, p. 17, 18. I highly recommend David K. Spurbeck's book, *The Christian "in Christ"*. See page 18 for publisher's information or go to: www.Ratzlaf.com and click on books for further information.

The Father's right hand is the command center for the Christian life

CHAPTER Eleven

KNOW THE "IN" AND "WITH" CHRIST TRUTHS

In the last chapter we learned that we died, were buried, were resurrected, and raised up "with Christ" and seated "with Christ" at the Father's right hand.

> But God, being rich in mercy, because of His great love with which He loved us, even when we were dead in our transgressions, made us alive together with Christ (by grace you have been saved), and raised us up with Him, and seated us with Him in the heavenly *places* in Christ Jesus (Eph. 2:4-6).

We also discovered the way to access these truths is by continually setting our mind on the things of the Spirit—the "in" and "with" Christ truths, declarations, and promises of God.

> Set your mind on the things above, not on the things that are on earth. For you have died and your life is hidden with Christ in God (Col. 3:2-3).

In Romans 8 Paul admonishes us to set our mind on the things of the Spirit.

> For the mind set on the flesh is death, but the mind set on the Spirit is life and peace, because the mind set on the flesh is hostile toward God; for it does not subject itself to the law of God, for it is not even able *to do so*, (Rom. 8:6-7).

Therefore, as we search out these "in Christ" truths realize that they are more than points on an outline. They are to be underlined in our thinking. We are to mediate upon them; ask questions of them; look at them from several viewpoints. As we affirm biblical truth the Holy Spirit will work out the fruit of the Spirit in our lives.

> For it is God who is at work in you, both to will and to work for *His* good pleasure (Phil. 2:13).

> But the fruit of the Spirit is love, joy, peace, patience, kindness, goodness, faithfulness, gentleness, self-control; against such things there is no law (Gal. 5:22-23).

Before we can apply the many "in Christ" truths to our lives, we must know what they are. We have broached these previously in our study now we will list them.

I am now under no condemnation.

> Therefore there is now no condemnation for those who are in Christ Jesus (Rom 8:1).

According to Scripture we all will continue to fall short of God's ideal.[60] When we do we often condemn ourselves for our shortcomings. However, this promise follows *immediately* after Paul's statements of failure recorded in Romans 7 when he took his eyes off of who he was "in Christ" and put them on his own behavior as measured by the law. Therefore, even in the presence of failure this promise holds. There is now no condemnation to those who are in Christ!

I now have received all of God's grace.

> To the praise of the glory of His grace, which He freely bestowed on us in the Beloved (Eph. 1:6).

When faced with difficulties I used to pray for more grace. However, now that I understand who I am "in Christ" I don't ask for more grace because He has already given me "all grace". I just ask to experience the boundless grace He has already given me.

---

[60] Rom. 3:23.

For the Law was given through Moses; grace and truth were realized through Jesus Christ (Jn. 1:17).

I thank my God always concerning you for the grace of God which was given you in Christ Jesus (1 Cor. 1:4).

But God, being rich in mercy, because of His great love with which He loved us, even when we were dead in our transgressions, made us alive together with Christ (by grace you have been saved (Eph. 2:4,5).

So that in the ages to come He might show the surpassing riches of His grace in kindness toward us in Christ Jesus (Eph. 2:7).

And God is able to make ***all grace*** abound to you, so that always having all sufficiency in everything, you may have an abundance for every good deed (2 Cor. 9:8).

I now have been brought near to God by the blood of Christ.

But now in Christ Jesus you who formerly were far off have been **brought near by the blood of Christ**. For He Himself is our peace, who made both *groups into* one and broke down the barrier of the dividing wall, by abolishing in His flesh the enmity, *which is* the Law of commandments *contained* in ordinances, so that in Himself He might make the two into one new man, *thus* establishing peace, and might reconcile them both in one body to God through the cross, by it having put to death the enmity (Eph. 2:13-16).

Have you ever felt that you were far from God? I have and I would judge that most readers of this little book have also at times experienced "a distant God". Just to think that we, sinners, can have bold confidence to come into the presence of God is unbelievable, but God's word says it is true.

> In whom we have boldness and **confident access through faith in Him** (Eph. 3:12).
>
> Therefore, brethren, since we have confidence to enter the holy place by the blood of Jesus, by a new and living way which He inaugurated for us through the veil, that is, His flesh, and since *we have* a great priest over the house of God, **let us draw near** with a sincere heart **in full assurance of faith**, having our hearts sprinkled *clean* from an evil conscience and our bodies washed with pure water (Heb. 10:19-22).

I am now a new creature in Christ and am part of a new creation which is His church.[61]

> Therefore if anyone is in Christ, *he is* a new creature; the old things passed away; behold, new things have come (2 Cor. 5:17).

More takes place in the moment we trust our lives to Christ after we hear the gospel than we can imagine. In that instant our spirits are regenerated and we are placed into a new group—the church—with all other believing Christians.

> For we are His workmanship, created in Christ Jesus for good works, which God prepared beforehand so that we would walk in them (Eph. 2:10).
>
> For neither is circumcision anything, nor uncircumcision, but a new creation (Gal. 6:15).
>
> For you are all sons of God through faith in Christ Jesus. For all of you who were baptized into Christ have clothed yourselves with Christ. There is neither Jew nor Greek, there is neither slave nor free man, there is neither male nor female; for you are all one in Christ Jesus. And if you belong to Christ, then you are Abraham's descendants, heirs according to promise (Gal. 3:26-29).

---

[61] The Greek simply says, "Therefore if anyone is in Christ a new creation" (2 Cor. 5:17). Some scholars believe this refers to the individual Christian, others to the church.

I now have received every spiritual blessing "in Christ".

> Blessed *be* the God and Father of our Lord Jesus Christ, who has blessed us with every spiritual blessing in the heavenly *places* in Christ (Eph. 1:3).

Meditate on this "in Christ" truth. Make a mental list of the spiritual blessings you need. Then read it again with believing and trusting faith.

I am now part of a holy priesthood offering spiritual sacrifices of praise to God and serving others.

> And coming to Him as to a living stone which has been rejected by men, but is choice and precious in the sight of God, you also, as living stones, are being built up as a spiritual house for a holy priesthood, to offer up spiritual sacrifices acceptable to God through Jesus Christ. But you are A CHOSEN RACE, A royal PRIESTHOOD, A HOLY NATION, A PEOPLE FOR *God's* OWN POSSESSION, so that you may proclaim the excellences of Him who has called you out of darkness into His marvelous light (1 Pet. 2:4,5,9).

> Through Him then, let us continually offer up a sacrifice of praise to God, that is, the fruit of lips that give thanks to His name. And do not neglect doing good and sharing, for with such sacrifices God is pleased (Heb. 13:15-16).

I am now justified, acquitted from all sin.

...being justified as a gift by His grace through the redemption which is in Christ Jesus; (Rom. 3:24).

I now have the very righteousness of God credited to my account.

He made Him who knew no sin *to be* sin on our behalf, so that we might become the righteousness of God in Him (2 Cor. 5:21).

Many of us have struggled for years trying to develop enough righteousness to be pleasing to God. Yes, and if you are like me, you failed. To believe these references that we are counted as having the very righteousness of God is good news indeed!

But **by His doing** you are in Christ Jesus, who became to us wisdom from God, and righteousness and sanctification, and redemption (1 Cor. 1:30).

...and may be found in Him, not having a righteousness of my own derived from *the* Law, but that which is through faith in Christ, the righteousness which *comes* from God on the basis of faith (Phil. 3:9).

I am now redeemed from the slavery of sin.

Being justified as a gift by His grace through the redemption which is in Christ Jesus (Rom 3:24).

I am now reconciled to God.

For if while we were enemies we were reconciled to God through the death of His Son, much more, having been reconciled, we shall be saved by His life (Rom. 5:10).

I am now at peace with God.

Therefore, having been justified by faith, we have peace with God through our Lord Jesus Christ (Rom 5:1).

I am now sanctified, perfected, and set apart.

By this will we have been sanctified through the offering of the body of Jesus Christ once for all...For by one offering He has perfected for all time those who are sanctified (Heb. 10:10,14).

Look carefully at the above verse. Christ's "one offering" has perfected us for all time.

I am now free from the law of sin and death.

For the law of the Spirit of life in Christ Jesus has set you free from the law of sin and of death (Rom. 8:2).

This was done the very instant we trusted Christ.

I am now a dwelling for the Spirit of God.

> In whom the whole building, being fitted together, is growing into a holy temple in the Lord, in whom you also are being built together into a dwelling of God in the Spirit (Eph. 2:21-22).
>
> However, you are not in the flesh but in the Spirit, if indeed the Spirit of God dwells in you. But if anyone does not have the Spirit of Christ, he does not belong to Him. If Christ is in you, though the body is dead because of sin, yet the spirit is alive because of righteousness (Rom. 8:9-10).

I am now sealed by the Holy Spirit.

> In Him, you also, after listening to the message of truth, the gospel of your salvation—having also believed, you were sealed in Him with the Holy Spirit of promise, who is given as a pledge of our inheritance, with a view to the redemption of *God's own* possession, to the praise of His glory (Eph. 1:13-14).

Notice that the sealing is not something we do, nor is it something we get when we have reached a degree of perfection. We are sealed the instant we are placed in Christ. This seal is the guarantee of our inheritance.

I now have received a spiritual gift.

> For by one Spirit we were all baptized into one body, whether Jews or Greeks, whether slaves or free, and we were all made to drink of one Spirit (1 Cor. 12:13).

> But now God has placed the members, each one of them, in the body, just as He desired (1 Cor. 12:18).

> For just as we have many members in one body and all the members do not have the same function, so we, who are many, are one body in Christ, and individually members one of another. Since we have gifts that differ according to the grace given to us, *each of us is to exercise them accordingly*: if prophecy, according to the proportion of his faith; if service, in his serving; or he who teaches, in his teaching; or he who exhorts, in his exhortation; he who gives, with liberality; he who leads, with diligence; he who shows mercy, with cheerfulness (Rom. 12:4-8).

As we become involved in the church and attend home Bible study and fellowship groups we should be able to discern which of the spiritual gifts we possess. When we serve God through our spiritual gift we have motivation and fulfillment in our Christian walk.

I now have liberty in Christ.

> But *it was* because of the false brethren secretly brought in, who had sneaked in to spy out our liberty which we have in Christ Jesus, in order to bring us into bondage (Gal. 2:4).

In our ministry I am often told that if we don't run our lives by continually looking at the law, that Christian liberty will soon become license and lead into sin. Nothing could be further from the truth.

> Now the Lord is the Spirit, and where the Spirit of the Lord is, *there* is liberty. But we all, with unveiled face, beholding as in a mirror the glory of the Lord, are being transformed into the same image from glory to glory, just as from the Lord, the Spirit (2 Cor. 3:17-18).

I am now a mature child of God.

> For you are all sons of God through faith in Christ Jesus. For all of you who were baptized into Christ have clothed yourselves with Christ. There is neither Jew nor Greek, there is neither slave nor free man, there is neither male nor female; for you are all one in Christ Jesus (Gal. 3:26-28).

> Now I say, as long as the heir is a child, he does not differ at all from a slave although he is owner of everything, but he is under guardians and managers until the date set by the father. So also we, while we were children, were held in bondage

> under the elemental things of the world. But when the fullness of the time came, God sent forth His Son, born of a woman, born under the Law, so that He might redeem those who were under the Law, that we might receive the adoption as sons. Because you are sons, God has sent forth the Spirit of His Son into our hearts, crying, "Abba! Father!" Therefore you are no longer a slave, but a son; and if a son, then an heir through God (Gal. 4:1-7).

The Greek word for "son" implies a mature son; one who has the rights of inheritance.

I now have eternal life.

> Truly, truly, I say to you, he who believes has eternal life (Joh 6:47).

I now have passed once and for all out of the realm of death into the realm of life.

> Truly, truly, I say to you, he who hears My word, and believes Him who sent Me, has eternal life, and does not come into judgment, but has passed out of death into life (Jn. 5:24).

"Has passed" is perfect tense, indicating a permanent change. We have changed residences. We have moved from the condemned family of Adam into the justified family of Christ and are not moving back!

I now have entered God's rest.

> For we who have **believed** [aorist tense—it happened in a moment of time] enter that rest, just as He has said, "AS I SWORE IN MY WRATH, THEY SHALL NOT ENTER MY REST," although His works were finished from the foundation of the world (Heb. 4:3).

> Come to Me, all who are weary and heavy-laden, and I will **give** you rest. Take My yoke upon you and learn from Me, for I am gentle and humble in heart, and YOU WILL FIND REST FOR YOUR SOULS. For My yoke is easy and My burden is light (Mt. 11:28-30).

Through the gospel Jesus brings the true, Sabbath-like rest "today" which is the reality to which the Jewish Sabbath pointed. We enter that rest of God by believing, the moment we are placed into Christ.

I am now freed from sin.

> But now having been freed from sin and enslaved to God, you derive your benefit, resulting in sanctification, and the outcome, eternal life (Rom. 6:22).

I am now dead to sin.

> Even so consider yourselves to be dead to sin, but alive to God in Christ Jesus (Rom. 6:11).

I am now free from the law.

> But now we have been released from the Law, having died to that by which we were bound, so that we serve in newness of the Spirit and not in oldness of the letter (Rom. 7:6).

When correctly understood, this is the secret to living a life where there is no condemnation and one which will ultimately develop harmony with God's moral principles.

I am now adopted into God's family.

> For you have not received a spirit of slavery leading to fear again, but you have received a spirit of adoption as sons by which we cry out, "Abba! Father!" (Rom 8:15).

I am now qualified to share the inheritance of the saints in light.

> ...giving thanks to the Father, who has qualified us to share in the inheritance of the saints in Light (Col. 1:12).

These are not all the gospel truths and precious promises of God's word, and I encourage you to add to these as you read through the New Testament. However these will serve you well as you make them your personal affirmation as outlined in the next chapter.

I have been a Christian for many years, but I never realized before how much God loves me!

CHAPTER Twelve

AFFIRM GOSPEL TRUTH

Danger in personal affirmations

Much has been written about the value of personal affirmations. Self-improvement books, personal training, and courses on success have illustrated and confirmed their value. The old classic, *Think and Grow Rich* by Napoleon Hill, is an example. Many successful leaders apply these principles on a regular basis. However, for the Christian there is danger here. Many of the examples in the self-improvement books are designed to help one achieve personal wealth, power, influence, and success. While there is nothing wrong with any of these as such, as Christians we must be very careful of three things. (1) Is our *goal* compatible with biblical values? Are we striving toward a Christian "worthy ideal"? (2) Do our *plans* to reach our desired goal include *only* the activities that reflect the morality and integrity of Christian character? (3) Do we sense a *call of God*, a spiritual motivation, to pursue our goal *knowing* we are in the will of God? If we cannot answer affirmatively to all three of these, then our self-made affirmations may lead us away from Christ and strengthen our selfishness which is the root of all sorts of evil.[62]

There is much value, however, in following the *right* path to holiness. And that path is to believe what God has declared about the believing Christian. We have stated this truth on several previous occasions and for good reason. ***It is the key to victory in the Christian life***. These "in" and "with" Christ truths, declarations, and magnificent and precious promises are to be ***our personal affirmations***. We know they are the will of God because they are the commands, declarations, and promises of Scripture.

In our Romans home Bible study group after completing chapter 8, each person was given the assignment to write out who he/she was "in Christ" using some 30 New Testament declarations. The next week the members of the group read these "gospel affirmations". There were few dry eyes as each member read or listened to the others read, who they are "in Christ". After one

[62] See 1 Tim. 6:10.

lady read her prepared statement, with tears in her eyes she said, "I have been a Christian for many years, but I never realized before how much God loves me!"

Personal affirmations of gospel truth

Using the "in" and "with" Christ truths and the magnificent promises listed in the last chapter,[63] write out a statement of who **you** are "in" and "with" Christ. Remember Abraham; God counted him righteous because he ***believed*** what God had ***declared***. We, too, are to focus our thinking on "things above"—the "in" and "with" Christ truths we have studied. These with the magnificent and precious promises of the New Testament are able to provide *everything* we need for life and godliness. That is the promise of His word![64]

Following are illustrations of what might be used as gospel affirmations. However, I highly recommend that you review the last chapter, and **write out your own statement** of who you now are "in Christ". The very act of doing this will prove to be a blessing to you. Remember, we believe because God has declared it so! I suggest

---

[63] You can add to these as you read through the New Testament looking for them.

[64] See 2 Pet. 2-4.

that after you have prepared your gospel affirmation that you read it often. Read it out loud when you wake up in the morning. Read it out loud before you go to sleep at night. As you do this, these gospel truths will transform your life.

Options and Illustrations

There are many ways one can apply what we have discovered regarding "in-Christ" truth. One can write out who they are in Christ as mentioned above. The statement could be short, listing only the truths you feel most relevant to your personal situation here and now. Read this every day for a week and then next week you could re-read the list of "in-Christ" truths and select others to consider for that week. Here is what one member of our home Bible study group wrote.

> In Christ I have been fully redeemed. Jesus died on the cross for me and for my sins. Now I am a new person and walking in a new life. I am clothed in Jesus' righteousness. I am dead to the power of sin and I am spiritually complete. In Christ I have been brought near to God, chosen to be holy and blameless with no condemnation. In Christ I am God's masterpiece. I am already seated in heavenly places at the right hand of God. In Christ I will be eternally in the presence of God. In Christ I am and always will be His beloved.

Another option would be to select just one or two "in-Christ" truths. Memorize the Scriptures upon which these are based, write them on a card or note pad and carry this with you for a week at a time. Meditate on this truth, ask questions of it, and pray about these truths. Teach them to someone else. Then, the next week select one or two other "in-Christ" truths and do the same with these.

For example if you grew up fearing the judgment as I did, and not knowing if you were good enough to meet Christ in peace, you might choose John 5:24 and Colossians 1:12 for this week's affirmation.

> Truly, truly, I say to you, he who hears My word, and believes Him who sent Me, has eternal life, and **does not come into judgment**, but **has passed out of death into life.**
>
> Giving thanks to the Father, **who has qualified us** to share in the inheritance of the saints in Light.

Remember to put these truths into ***personal*** affirmations.

> I now have eternal life and I will not come into judgment because I have already passed out of the realm of death into the realm of life. I know this is true because my Father has already qualified me to share in the inheritance of the saints in light.

After studying the book of Ephesians some years ago, here is what one person wrote.

> I was personally chosen by God the Father to be holy and blameless "in Christ". I have been adopted into the family of God with full rights of inheritance "in Christ". Christ has paid the redemption price to set me free from the controlling power of sin. Christ has forgiven all the guilt of all my sins. Christ has revealed to me that someday everyone and everything will submit to Christ's lordship—I am on the winning team! I have heard the word of truth. I have believed the good news of the gospel of salvation "in Christ". I have been sealed with the Holy Spirit who guarantees that I will receive the promised inheritance. Because of who I am "in Christ", I am equipped to handle the difficulties, pressures, problems, stresses, uncertainties, and disappointments that may come to me today. I know where I came from, why I am here, and where I am going. I have been blessed with every spiritual blessing in Christ Jesus! I am a child of the King to the praise of His glory!

Perhaps you would like to have your affirmation include as many of the "in" and "with" Christ truths as possible as this person did.

> I have heard and believed gospel truth that Christ died for my sin, was buried, was raised from the dead, and is now seated at the Father's right hand. Yes, and I was raised up with Christ so that

all the “in Christ” truths, declarations, and promises of the New Testament now apply to me. Therefore, I have freely received all of God’s grace and all my sins have been forgiven. I have been brought near to God by the blood of Christ. I am a new creature in Christ and I am a member of His new creation—the church. I have received every spiritual blessing in Christ. Now that I am in Christ I have the very righteousness of God credited to my account. In Christ Jesus I am sanctified and perfected. I am now a mature, beloved child of God with full rights of inheritance. My inheritance in the kingdom of light is guaranteed by the seal of the Holy Spirit which I received the moment I trusted Christ for salvation. I am now free from the law of sin and death. I am free from the law in that I died with Christ and the law’s ability to condemn me ended at the tomb. I am dead to sin; yes, I am free from sin in Christ. I am a dwelling for the Holy Spirit therefore I have liberty to follow God’s plan for my life. I am no longer fearful of the judgment because I have passed once and for all out of the realm of death into the realm of life. Christ was judged, condemned, and suffered the wrath that should have been mine. I am no longer fearful of death because I *now* have eternal life in Christ. I have been reconciled to God and now can experience peace with God and can live victoriously in the peace of God. I have received a spiritual gift and desire to use it in loving fellowship with other Christians. When I see other Christians sinning I will

> no longer gossip, but will help them to know who they are, or can be, "in Christ Jesus." I will continue to review the many blessings of the gospel and in so doing I know that the Holy Spirit will work out in my life the fruit of the Spirit.

As you continue to affirm gospel truth, over time you will be renewing your mind as you allow the Holy Spirit to create your "new self" in Christ Jesus.[65]

When I was doing an in-depth study of Romans 3:21-26, I memorized this section and when I took my daily walk or run I would repeat this wonderful passage. I would consider each point, pray about it, and relish in the gospel of God's matchless grace. It is a life-changing passage.

At the conclusion of this book we have included a page that you may copy or cut out as you wish. This page numbers 27 of the "in Christ" truths in summary form. We suggest that you use a numbered memory-hook system[66] so that you can easily recall these life-transforming truths. Then throughout the day you can go over them, meditate on each one. Thank God for the transforming gospel that He has so freely bestowed on us poor sinners!

---

[65] Eph. 4:24; Col. 3:10.

[66] You can find several on Google, or in books on memory.

Strive **to be who you** ***now*** **are "in Christ"**

Thus far we have given little attention to the idea of striving in the Christian life. However, Scripture in many places speaks of Christians striving in their battle with sin and the flesh.[67] The admonitions to a changed lifestyle, however, come *after* a thorough presentation of the gospel, lest we fall back into trusting our good behavior—which is never good enough—for our acceptance with God. Paul gives an illustrative description in his fight with self.

> Therefore I run in such a way, as not without aim; I box in such a way, as not beating the air; but I discipline my body and make it my slave, so that, after I have preached to others, I myself will not be disqualified (1 Cor. 9:26-27).

The passage listed below is a very important verse dealing with the process of sanctification. I am listing this passage from the New English Translation as I believe the New American Standard Bible is incorrect in its rendering of Romans 8:10. I have added my comments and/or interpretation in brackets in the passage below.

> Those who are in the flesh cannot please God. You, however, are not in the flesh but in the Spirit,

---

[67] See Lk. 13:25; 1 Tim. 4:10; Heb. 12:4.

> if indeed the Spirit of God lives in you. Now if anyone does not have the Spirit of Christ, this person does not belong to him. But if Christ is in you, your body is [spiritually] dead because of sin, but the Spirit is your life because of [Christ's] righteousness [imputed to you]. Moreover if the Spirit of the one who raised Jesus from the dead lives in you, the one who raised Christ from the dead will also make your mortal bodies [spiritually] alive through his Spirit who lives in you. So then, brothers and sisters, we are under obligation, not to the flesh, to [continually] live according to the flesh (for if you [continually] live according to the flesh, you will [spiritually] die), but if **by the Spirit** [the active Agent in sanctification] **you** [continually] put to death the deeds of the body you will [spiritually] live (Rom. 8:8-13).

By adding "continually" I am in essence giving a secondary interpretation to this text. Many hold that Paul is primarily showing what will be the end result of those who "live according to the flesh." Nevertheless, this verse also has a direct application to us here and now.

This insightful passage teaches us that even though we live in a body that has a sinful nature, by **cooperating** with the indwelling Holy Spirit we can continually put to death the deeds of the flesh. We no longer owe a debt to our sinful nature to carry out the ongoing sin that is prompted by this nature.

The question comes again. *How* do we cooperate with the Holy Spirit who is the active agent, the power in life change? We have already stated that it is to affirm the truth of who we now are “in” and “with” Christ. Lest some read into this the idea that there is nothing else for us to do, I want to expand on this truth. Not only are we to affirm biblical truth, we are to **strive** to be the person we **now are** “in” and “with” Christ. It is not enough just to **say** I am a child of God, we are also to **strive** to live like a child of God. And this will hold true for every one of the “in” and “with” Christ truths. Therefore as we rehearse each of these biblical affirmations let us ask God to show us any changes that need to be made in our lives in order to **be** more like who we **now are** “in Christ”. I have at times likened this to running in a race holding in our pocket the winning trophy. We may stumble, even fall, in the footrace of life, but all the while we cling to the winning trophy. The fact that “in Christ” we have **already** won, removes any condemnation when we stumble or fall. We are complete “in Him” and this ongoing state remains until we meet Him in glory.

Affirm gospel truth with thanksgiving

As we read and meditate on the many "in-Christ" truths in our personal affirmations, we are not trying to make ourselves believe what is not true as many of the success programs do. Rather because these affirmations are based upon the truths of God's word, we affirm gospel truth to counter the many lies springing from our own sinful nature, worldly influences, and deceptions of Satan.

When we review our gospel affirmations we contemplate the great love and sacrifice Christ made for us. As we understand more of the depths of God's love in our salvation our hearts melt with gratitude and joy. We can echo Paul's songs of praise and thanksgiving.

> ...that He would grant you, according to the riches of His glory, to be strengthened with power through His Spirit in the inner man, so that Christ may dwell in your hearts through faith; *and* that you, being rooted and grounded in love, may be able to comprehend with all the saints what is the breadth and length and height and depth, and to know the love of Christ which surpasses knowledge, that you may be filled up to all the fullness of God. Now to Him who is able to do far more abundantly beyond all that we ask or think,

according to the power that works within us. (Eph. 3:16-20).

Be anxious for nothing, but in everything by prayer and supplication with thanksgiving let your requests be made known to God. And the peace of God, which surpasses all comprehension, will guard your hearts and your minds in Christ Jesus. Finally, brethren, whatever is true, whatever is honorable, whatever is right, whatever is pure, whatever is lovely, whatever is of good repute, if there is any excellence and if anything worthy of praise, dwell on these things (Phil. 4:6-8).

Gospel transformation in "one another" ministry

Can you imagine a Christian fellowship where if one believer sees another believer living in sin, instead of gossiping, he goes to the sinning believer and helps that person understand who he is "in" and "with" Christ and then helps him live that way? Could it be that the same path to holiness that works *for us* would work in a sinning brother or sister? Could an in-depth understanding of the gospel *by each and every church member* be the catalyst to foster true, loving "one another" ministry in church or group settings? Why not start practicing gospel transformation and then share it with others? There are many discouraged church members who only put on a front of a peaceful life. Inside they are full of guilt and frustration thinking they can never be good enough. Now, you are in a position to help them.

Yes, gospel transformation is gazing at the glory of the gospel. By so doing we are being ***transformed*** into God's image by the Holy Spirit.

> Therefore having such a hope, we use great boldness in *our* speech, and *are* not like Moses, *who* used to put a veil over his face so that the sons of Israel would not look intently at the end of what was fading away. But their minds were hardened; for until this very day at the reading of the old covenant the same veil remains unlifted, because it is removed in Christ. But to this day whenever Moses is read, a veil lies over their heart; but whenever a person turns to the Lord, the veil is taken away. Now the Lord is the Spirit, and where the Spirit of the Lord is, *there* is liberty. **But we all, with unveiled face, *beholding* as in a mirror the glory of the Lord, are being *transformed* into the same image from glory to glory, just as from the Lord, the Spirit** (2 Cor. 3:12-18).

Who I now am "in Christ"

"I believe it because God's word declares it"

1. I am now under no condemnation.
2. I now have received all of God's grace.
3. I now have been brought near to God by the blood of Christ.
4. I am now a new creature in Christ Jesus.
5. I am now part of a new creation which is Christ's church.
6. I now have received every spiritual blessing "in Christ".
7. I am now part of a holy priesthood offering spiritual sacrifices of praise to God and serving others.
8. I am now justified and acquitted from all sin.
9. I now have the very righteousness of God credited to my account.
10. I am now redeemed from the slavery of sin.
11. I am now reconciled to God.
12. I now have peace with God.
13. I am now sanctified, perfected, and set apart in Christ.
14. I am now free from the law of sin and death.
15. I am now a dwelling for the Spirit of God.
16. I am now sealed by the Holy Spirit who guarantees my inheritance.
17. I now have received a spiritual gift.
18. I now have liberty in Christ.
19. I now have eternal life.
20. I now have once and for all passed out of the realm of death into the realm of life.
21. I now have entered God's rest.
22. I am now freed from sin.
23. I am now dead to sin.
24. I am now free from the law.
25. I am now adopted into God's family.
26. I am now a mature child of God.
27. I am now qualified to share the inheritance of the saints in light.

This and the following pages are for you to add other "in" and "with" Christ truths and magnificent and precious promises made to believing Christians. You will find these as you read through the New Testament. Enter the "truth" or "promise" and the Bible reference and add them to your gospel affirmations.